MW01283812

Learning Selenium Testing Tools with Python

A practical guide on automated web testing with Selenium using Python

Unmesh Gundecha

[PACKT] open source ✳
PUBLISHING   community experience distilled

BIRMINGHAM - MUMBAI

Learning Selenium Testing Tools with Python

Copyright © 2014 Packt Publishing

All rights reserved. No part of this book may be reproduced, stored in a retrieval system, or transmitted in any form or by any means, without the prior written permission of the publisher, except in the case of brief quotations embedded in critical articles or reviews.

Every effort has been made in the preparation of this book to ensure the accuracy of the information presented. However, the information contained in this book is sold without warranty, either express or implied. Neither the author, nor Packt Publishing, and its dealers and distributors will be held liable for any damages caused or alleged to be caused directly or indirectly by this book.

Packt Publishing has endeavored to provide trademark information about all of the companies and products mentioned in this book by the appropriate use of capitals. However, Packt Publishing cannot guarantee the accuracy of this information.

First published: December 2014

Production reference: 1231214

Published by Packt Publishing Ltd.
Livery Place
35 Livery Street
Birmingham B3 2PB, UK.

ISBN 978-1-78398-350-6

www.packtpub.com

Credits

Author
Unmesh Gundecha

Reviewers
Adil Imroz
Dr. Philip Polstra
Walt Stoneburner
Yuri Weinstein

Commissioning Editor
Usha Iyer

Acquisition Editor
Neha Nagwekar

Content Development Editor
Athira Laji

Technical Editor
Mrunmayee Patil

Copy Editor
Laxmi Subramanian

Project Coordinator
Harshal Ved

Proofreaders
Ameesha Green
Chris Smith

Indexer
Monica Ajmera Mehta

Production Coordinator
Nilesh R. Mohite

Cover Work
Nilesh R. Mohite

About the Author

Unmesh Gundecha has a Master's degree in Software Engineering and over 12 years of experience in software development and testing. Unmesh has architected functional test automation solutions using industry standards, in-house and custom test automation frameworks along with leading commercial and open source test automation tools.

He has development experience in Microsoft technologies and Java. He is presently working as a test solution architect with a multinational company in Pune, India.

His experience includes support to Ruby, Java, iOS, Android, and PHP projects as an automated tester and software developer.

He authored *Selenium Testing Tools Cookbook*, *Packt Publishing* in November 2012.

I would like to thank Neha Nagwekar, acquisition editor, for giving me an opportunity to write this book; Athira Laji, content development editor; Harshal Ved, project coordinator, for constantly supporting and encouraging me in completing this book; and the entire team at Packt Publishing.

This book has benefited a lot from a great team of technical reviewers. I'd like to thank each of them for volunteering their time reviewing the drafts of this book and providing valuable feedback.

I would also like to thank my mentor and friend, Yuri Weinstein, for his support and help during this project. Thanks to my friends and colleagues at work for their constant encouragement and support in writing this book.

About the Reviewers

Adil Imroz is a Python enthusiast who loves the simplicity of this beautiful language. He is a software developer in testing by profession and a mobile automation expert. He likes playing around with open source software and believes in being agile. When not working, he can be found biking, reading a book, or sleeping. He believes that there is a lot of scope around; all you have to do is hit the right chords. You can get in touch with him via e-mail at `alam.adil12@gmail.com`. You can also follow him on Twitter at `@adilimroz`.

Dr. Philip Polstra (known to his friends as Dr. Phil) is an internationally recognized hardware hacker. His work has been presented at numerous conferences around the globe, including repeat performances at DEFCON, Black Hat, 44CON, Maker Faire, and other top conferences. Dr. Polstra is a well-known expert on USB forensics and has published several articles on this topic.

Recently, Dr. Polstra has developed a penetration testing Linux distribution, known as The Deck, for the BeagleBone and BeagleBoard family of small computer boards. He has also developed a new way of performing penetration testing with multiple low-power devices, including an aerial hacking drone. This work is described in his book *Hacking and Penetration Testing with Low Power Devices*, *Syngress Media* (2014). Dr. Polstra has also been a technical reviewer on several books, including *BeagleBone Home Automation* by Juha Lumme and *BeagleBone for Secret Agents* by Josh Datko, both published in 2014 by Packt Publishing.

Dr. Polstra is an Associate Professor at Bloomsburg University of Pennsylvania (`http://bloomu.edu/digital_forensics`), where he teaches digital forensics among other topics. In addition to teaching, he provides training and performs penetration tests on a consulting basis. When not working, he is known to fly, build aircraft, and tinker with electronics. His latest happenings can be found on his blog at `http://philpolstra.com`. You can also follow him on Twitter at `@ppolstra`.

Walt Stoneburner is a software architect with over 25 years of commercial application development and consulting experience. His fringe passions involve quality assurance, configuration management, and security. If cornered, he may actually admit to liking statistics and authoring documentation as well.

He's easily amused by programming language design, collaborative applications, big data, knowledge management, data visualization, and ASCII art. A self-proclaimed closet geek, Walt also evaluates software products and consumer electronics, draws cartoons, runs a freelance photography studio specializing in portraits and art (`http://charismaticmoments.com/`), writes humor pieces, performs sleight of hand, enjoys game designing, and can occasionally be found on ham radio.

Walt can be reached directly via e-mail at `wls@wwco.com` or `Walt.Stoneburner@gmail.com`. He publishes a tech and humor blog called *Walt-O-Matic* at `https://www.wwco.com/~wls/blog/`.

His other book reviews and contributions include the following:

- *AntiPatterns and Patterns in Software Configuration Management*, John Wiley & Sons (ISBN 978-0471329299, p. xi)

- *Exploiting Software: How to Break Code*, Pearson Education (ISBN 978-0-201-78695-8, p. xxxiii)

- *Ruby on Rails Web Mashup Projects*, Packt Publishing (ISBN 978-1847193933)

- *Building Dynamic Web 2.0 Websites with Ruby on Rails*, Packt Publishing (ISBN 978-1-847193-41-4)

- *Instant Sinatra Starter*, Packt Publishing (ISBN 978-1782168218)

- *C++ Multithreading Cookbook*, Packt Publishing (ISBN 978-1-78328-979-0)

- *Trapped in Whittier (A Trent Walker Thriller Book 1)*, Amazon Digital South Asia Services, Inc. (ASIN B00GTD1RBS)

- *South Mouth: Hillbilly Wisdom, Redneck Observations & Good Ol' Boy Logic*, CreateSpace Independent Publishing Platform (ISBN 978-1-482340-99-0)

Yuri Weinstein lives in San Francisco, CA with his family. He has spent over two decades working for top technology companies in the Silicon Valley, focusing on software testing with a special passion for test automation techniques. He currently works at Red Hat, ensuring the quality of the Ceph open source storage project.

www.PacktPub.com

Support files, eBooks, discount offers, and more

For support files and downloads related to your book, please visit www.PacktPub.com.

Did you know that Packt offers eBook versions of every book published, with PDF and ePub files available? You can upgrade to the eBook version at www.PacktPub.com and as a print book customer, you are entitled to a discount on the eBook copy. Get in touch with us at service@packtpub.com for more details.

At www.PacktPub.com, you can also read a collection of free technical articles, sign up for a range of free newsletters and receive exclusive discounts and offers on Packt books and eBooks.

https://www.packtpub.com/books/subscription/packtlib

Do you need instant solutions to your IT questions? PacktLib is Packt's online digital book library. Here, you can search, access, and read Packt's entire library of books.

Why subscribe?

- Fully searchable across every book published by Packt
- Copy and paste, print, and bookmark content
- On demand and accessible via a web browser

Free access for Packt account holders

If you have an account with Packt at www.PacktPub.com, you can use this to access PacktLib today and view 9 entirely free books. Simply use your login credentials for immediate access.

Table of Contents

Preface

Selenium is a set of tools for automating browsers. It is largely used for testing applications, but its usages are not limited only to testing. It can also be used for screen scraping and automating repetitive tasks in a browser window. Selenium supports automation on all the major browsers including Firefox, Internet Explorer, Google Chrome, Safari, and Opera. Selenium WebDriver is now a part of W3C standards and is supported by major browser vendors.

Selenium offers the following set of tools for automating interaction with browsers:

- **Selenium IDE**: This is a Firefox add-in used to record and play back the Selenium scripts with Firefox. It provides a graphical user interface to record user actions using Firefox. It is a great tool to start learning and using Selenium, but it can only be used with Firefox and other browsers are not supported. However, it can convert the recorded scripts into various programming languages supported by Selenium WebDriver, which supports running scripts on browsers other than Firefox.

- **Selenium WebDriver**: This is a programming interface for developing advanced Selenium scripts using programming languages. We can also run tests on multiple browsers that are supported by Selenium on multiple operating systems, including Linux, Windows, and Mac OS X. This makes Selenium a true cross-browser testing tool. Selenium WebDriver offers client libraries in various languages, including Java, C#, Python, Ruby, PHP, and JavaScript, and are more into writing test scripts.

- **Selenium standalone server**: This is also known as Selenium Grid and allows remote and distributed execution of Selenium scripts created with WebDriver. We can also use the grid feature of the standalone server to run tests in parallel, including tests on mobile platforms such as Android or Apple iOS for iPhone and iPad.

As the title suggests, this book will introduce you to the Selenium WebDriver client library for Python. You will learn how to use Selenium WebDriver in Python to automate browsers for testing web applications. This book contains lessons right from setting up Selenium to using the basic and advanced features of Selenium to create and run automated scripts for testing web applications. This book assumes you have a basic idea of programming using Python.

What this book covers

Chapter 1, Getting Started with Selenium WebDriver and Python, starts with installing Python and the Selenium WebDriver client library. We will select a Python editor or IDE for Selenium script development. We will then create our first automation script for a simple search workflow from the application under test. At the end of this chapter, we will run the Selenium script on various browsers supported by Selenium.

Chapter 2, Writing Tests Using unittest, shows you how to use Selenium and the unittest library to test web applications. We will convert the script into a unittest test case. We will create few more tests using Selenium and unittest. We will create a TestSuite for a group of tests. We will run these tests and analyze the results. At the end of this chapter, you will learn how to produce test reports in the HTML format that you can distribute to various stakeholders of the project.

Chapter 3, Finding Elements, introduces you to locators that are the keys to automate different types of User Interface (UI) elements displayed on the web pages in the browser window. Selenium uses locators to find elements on a page and then performs actions or retrieves their properties for testing. You will learn various methods to locate elements, including XPath and CSS. We will show you how to use these methods with examples on the application under test.

Chapter 4, Using the Selenium Python API for Element Interaction, shows you how to use the Selenium WebDriver client library to interact with different types of elements, JavaScript alerts, frames, and windows in Python. You will learn how to perform actions such as sending values to elements, performing clicks, and selecting options from dropdowns. You will also see how to handle frames, different types of JavaScript alerts, and switch between child browser windows.

Chapter 5, Synchronizing Tests, introduces you to various wait methods provided by Selenium to synchronize tests for reliable and robust execution. You will learn how to use the implicit and explicit wait to implement synchronization in Selenium tests. You will learn various methods to implement explicit wait in our test scripts.

Chapter 6, Cross-browser Testing, dives into using RemoteWebDriver to run cross-browser tests on remote machines or through the Selenium Grid. You will learn how to use RemoteWebDriver to run tests on remote machines. We will also set up a Selenium Grid to run tests on various combinations of browsers and operating systems. You will also see how to execute tests on headless browsers such as PhantomJS. At the end of the chapter, we will see how to use cloud testing tools such as Sauce Labs and BrowserStack to run tests in cloud using RemoteWebDriver.

Chapter 7, Testing on Mobile, shows you how to test applications on mobile devices using Selenium WebDriver and Appium. We will set up Appium to test our sample application on iOS and on an Android emulator and device. You will also learn how to run native mobile applications using Appium.

Chapter 8, Page Objects and Data-driven Testing, introduces you to two important design patterns to implement a maintainable and efficient testing framework. You will learn how to use page objects to hide the technical details of locators, and divide operations on pages into separate classes and create test cases that are more readable and easy to maintain. You will then learn how to create data-driven tests using the unittest library.

Chapter 9, Advanced Techniques of Selenium WebDriver, dives into some of the advanced techniques of using Selenium for automating browsers for testing. You will learn how to use various action methods for simulating complex mouse and keyboard operations using Selenium. You will see how to handle session cookies, capture screenshots during a test run, and create a movie of the entire test run.

Chapter 10, Integration with Other Tools and Frameworks, shows you how to use Selenium WebDriver with automated acceptance testing frameworks such as Behave and Continuous Integration tools. You will first learn how to integrate Selenium with Behave to create automated acceptance tests. We will implement a sample feature and acceptance tests on UI using the Selenium WebDriver. At end of the chapter, we will set up running the tests that we created as part of Continuous Integration using Jenkins. We will set up a schedule to run the tests on a daily frequency.

By the end of this book, you will have learned all the essential features of Selenium WebDriver to create your own web testing framework in Python.

What you need for this book

To get started with this book, you will need basic programming skills in Python as well as knowledge of web technologies such as HTML, JavaScript, CSS, and XML. If you are able to write a simple Python script, use loops and conditions, define classes, then you should be able to keep up with every example in this book. We will take the time to explain every line of code written in this book so that you are able to create the desired outcome in any situation you find yourself in. There are some software prerequisites that are needed, which are explained in the first chapter. You will need to have access to the command-line interface terminal, Python interpreter, and web browsers such as Firefox and Google Chrome on your machine. You can download and install Firefox from `https://www.mozilla.org/en-US/firefox/` and Google Chrome from `https://www.google.com/chrome/`. If you're a Windows user, you might be interested in testing Internet Explorer, which is installed by default with Windows.

Who this book is for

If you are a quality assurance/testing professional, software developer, or web application developer using Python and want to learn Selenium WebDriver to automate browsers for testing your web applications, this is the perfect guide for you to get started! As a prerequisite, this book expects you to have a basic understanding of the Python programming language, although any previous knowledge of Selenium WebDriver is not needed. By the end of this book, you will have acquired a comprehensive knowledge of Selenium WebDriver, which will help you in writing your automation tests.

Conventions

In this book, you will find a number of styles of text that distinguish between different kinds of information. Here are some examples of these styles, and an explanation of their meaning.

Code words in text, database table names, folder names, filenames, file extensions, pathnames, dummy URLs, user input, and Twitter handles are shown as follows: "The `pip` tool will download the latest version of the Selenium package and install it on your machine."

A block of code is set as follows:

```
# create a new Firefox session
driver = webdriver.Firefox()
driver.implicitly_wait(30)
driver.maximize_window()
```

When we wish to draw your attention to a particular part of a code block, the relevant lines or items are set in bold:

```
# run the suite
xmlrunner.XMLTestRunner(verbosity=2, output='test-reports').
  run(smoke_tests)
```

Any command-line input or output is written as follows:

```
pip install -U selenium
```

New terms and **important words** are shown in bold. Words that you see on the screen, in menus or dialog boxes for example, appear in the text like this: "Choose **Internet Options** from the **Tools** menu."

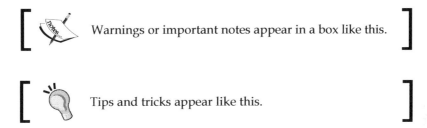

Warnings or important notes appear in a box like this.

Tips and tricks appear like this.

Reader feedback

Feedback from our readers is always welcome. Let us know what you think about this book—what you liked or disliked. Reader feedback is important for us as it helps us develop titles that you will really get the most out of.

To send us general feedback, simply e-mail feedback@packtpub.com, and mention the book's title in the subject of your message.

If there is a topic that you have expertise in and you are interested in either writing or contributing to a book, see our author guide at www.packtpub.com/authors.

Customer support

Now that you are the proud owner of a Packt book, we have a number of things to help you to get the most from your purchase.

Downloading the example code

You can download the example code files from your account at `http://www.packtpub.com` for all the Packt Publishing books you have purchased. If you purchased this book elsewhere, you can visit `http://www.packtpub.com/support` and register to have the files e-mailed directly to you.

Errata

Although we have taken every care to ensure the accuracy of our content, mistakes do happen. If you find a mistake in one of our books—maybe a mistake in the text or the code—we would be grateful if you could report this to us. By doing so, you can save other readers from frustration and help us improve subsequent versions of this book. If you find any errata, please report them by visiting `http://www.packtpub.com/submit-errata`, selecting your book, clicking on the **Errata Submission Form** link, and entering the details of your errata. Once your errata are verified, your submission will be accepted and the errata will be uploaded to our website or added to any list of existing errata under the Errata section of that title.

To view the previously submitted errata, go to `https://www.packtpub.com/books/content/support` and enter the name of the book in the search field. The required information will appear under the **Errata** section.

Piracy

Piracy of copyrighted material on the Internet is an ongoing problem across all media. At Packt, we take the protection of our copyright and licenses very seriously. If you come across any illegal copies of our works in any form on the Internet, please provide us with the location address or website name immediately so that we can pursue a remedy.

Please contact us at `copyright@packtpub.com` with a link to the suspected pirated material.

We appreciate your help in protecting our authors and our ability to bring you valuable content.

Questions

If you have a problem with any aspect of this book, you can contact us at `questions@packtpub.com`, and we will do our best to address the problem.

1
Getting Started with Selenium WebDriver and Python

Selenium automates browsers. It automates the interaction we do in a browser window such as navigating to a website, clicking on links, filling out forms, submitting forms, navigating through pages, and so on. It works on every major browser available out there.

In order to use Selenium WebDriver, we need a programing language to write automation scripts. The language that we select should also have a Selenium client library available.

In this book, we will use Python along with the Selenium WebDriver client library to create automated scripts. Python is a widely used general-purpose, high-level programming language. It's easy and its syntax allows us to express concepts in fewer lines of code. It emphasizes code readability and provides constructs that enable us to write programs on both the small and large scale. It also provides a number of in-built and user-written libraries to achieve complex tasks quite easily.

The Selenium WebDriver client library for Python provides access to all the Selenium WebDriver features and Selenium standalone server for remote and distributed testing of browser-based applications. Selenium Python language bindings are developed and maintained by David Burns, Adam Goucher, Maik Röder, Jason Huggins, Luke Semerau, Miki Tebeka, and Eric Allenin.

The Selenium WebDriver client library is supported on Python Version 2.6, 2.7, 3.2, and 3.3.

This chapter will introduce you to the Selenium WebDriver client library for Python by demonstrating its installation, basic features, and overall structure.

In this chapter, we will cover the following topics:

- Installing Python and Selenium package
- Selecting and setting up a Python editor
- Implementing a sample script using the Selenium WebDriver Python client library
- Implementing cross-browser support with Internet Explorer and Google Chrome

Preparing your machine

As a first step of using Selenium with Python, we'll need to install it on our computer with the minimum requirements possible. Let's set up the basic environment with the steps explained in the following sections.

Installing Python

You will find Python installed by default on most Linux distributions, Mac OS X, and other Unix machines. On Windows, you will need to install it separately. Installers for different platforms can be found at `http://python.org/download/`.

> All the examples in this book are written and tested on Python 2.7 and Python 3.0 on Windows 8 operating systems.

Installing the Selenium package

The Selenium WebDriver Python client library is available in the Selenium package. To install the Selenium package in a simple way, use the `pip` installer tool available at `https://pip.pypa.io/en/latest/`.

With `pip`, you can simply install or upgrade the Selenium package using the following command:

```
pip install -U selenium
```

This is a fairly simple process. This command will set up the Selenium WebDriver client library on your machine with all modules and classes that we will need to create automated scripts using Python. The `pip` tool will download the latest version of the Selenium package and install it on your machine. The optional `-U` flag will upgrade the existing version of the installed package to the latest version.

You can also download the latest version of the Selenium package source from `https://pypi.python.org/pypi/selenium`. Just click on the **Download** button on the upper-right-hand side of the page, unarchive the downloaded file, and install it with following command:

```
python setup.py install
```

Browsing the Selenium WebDriver Python documentation

The Selenium WebDriver Python client library documentation is available at `http://selenium.googlecode.com/git/docs/api/py/api.html` as shown in the following screenshot:

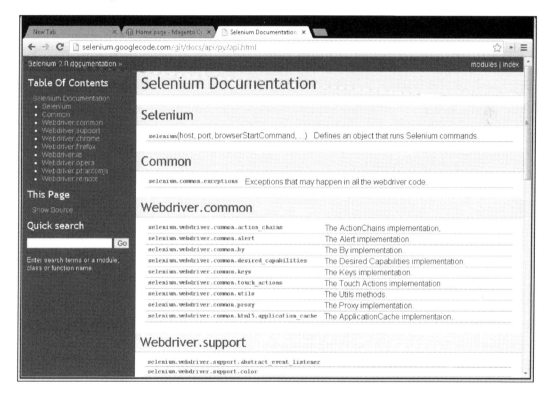

It offers detailed information on all core classes and functions of Selenium WebDriver. Also note the following links for Selenium documentation:

- The official documentation at `http://docs.seleniumhq.org/docs/` offers documentation for all the Selenium components with examples in supported languages

- Selenium Wiki at `https://code.google.com/p/selenium/w/list` lists some useful topics that we will explore later in this book

Selecting an IDE

Now that we have Python and Selenium WebDriver set up, we will need an editor or an **Integrated Development Environment (IDE)** to write automation scripts. A good editor or IDE increases the productivity and helps in doing a lot of other things that make the coding experience simple and easy. While we can write Python code in simple editors such as Emacs, Vim, or Notepad, using an IDE will make life a lot easier. There are many IDEs to choose from. Generally, an IDE provides the following features to accelerate your development and coding time:

- A graphical code editor with code completion and IntelliSense

- A code explorer for functions and classes

- Syntax highlighting

- Project management

- Code templates

- Tools for unit testing and debugging

- Source control support

If you're new to Python, or you're a tester working for the first time in Python, your development team will help you to set up the right IDE.

However, if you're starting with Python for the first time and don't know which IDE to select, here are a few choices that you might want to consider.

PyCharm

PyCharm is developed by JetBrains, a leading vendor of professional development tools and IDEs such as IntelliJ IDEA, RubyMine, PhpStorm, and TeamCity.

PyCharm is a polished, powerful, and versatile IDE that works pretty well. It brings best of the JetBrains experience in building powerful IDEs with lots of other features for a highly productive experience.

PyCharm is supported on Windows, Linux, and Mac. To know more about PyCharm and its features visit `http://www.jetbrains.com/pycharm/`.

PyCharm comes in two versions—a community edition and a professional edition. The community edition is free, whereas you have to pay for the professional edition. Here is the PyCharm community edition running a sample Selenium script in the following screenshot:

The community edition is great for building and running Selenium scripts with its fantastic debugging support. We will use PyCharm in the rest of this book. Later in this chapter, we will set up PyCharm and create our first Selenium script.

 All the examples in this book are built using PyCharm; however, you can easily use these examples in your choice of editor or IDE.

The PyDev Eclipse plugin

The PyDev Eclipse plugin is another widely used editor among Python developers. Eclipse is a famous open source IDE primarily built for Java; however, it also offers support to various other programming languages and tools through its powerful plugin architecture.

Eclipse is a cross-platform IDE supported on Windows, Linux, and Mac. You can get the latest edition of Eclipse at `http://www.eclipse.org/downloads/`.

You need to install the PyDev plugin separately after setting up Eclipse. Use the tutorial from *Lars Vogel* to install PyDev at `http://www.vogella.com/tutorials/Python/article.html` to install PyDev. Installation instructions are also available at `http://pydev.org/`.

Here's the Eclipse PyDev plugin running a sample Selenium script as shown in the following screenshot:

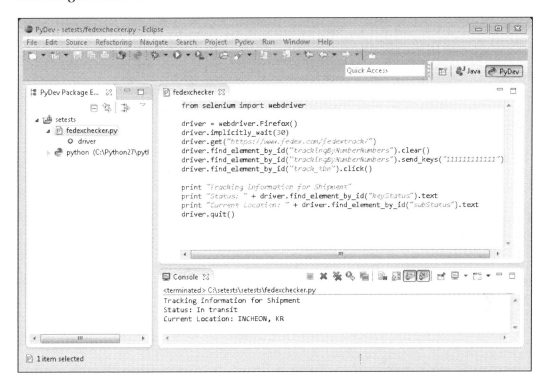

PyScripter

For the Windows users, PyScripter can also be a great choice. It is open source, lightweight, and provides all the features that modern IDEs offer such as IntelliSense and code completion, testing, and debugging support. You can find more about PyScripter along with its download information at `https://code.google.com/p/ pyscripter/`.

Here's PyScripter running a sample Selenium script as shown in the following screenshot:

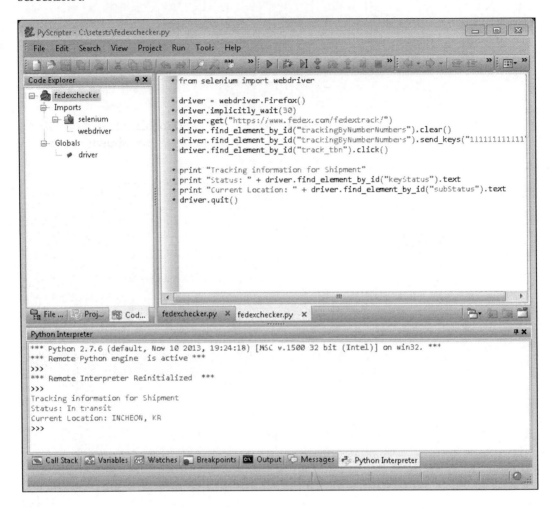

Setting up PyCharm

Now that we have seen IDE choices, let's set up PyCharm. All examples in this book are created with PyCharm. However, you can set up any other IDE of your choice and use examples as they are. We will set up PyCharm with following steps to get started with Selenium Python:

1. Download and install the PyCharm Community Edition from JetBrains site `http://www.jetbrains.com/pycharm/download/index.html`.

2. Launch the PyCharm Community Edition. Click on the **Create New Project** option on the **PyCharm Community Edition** dialog box as shown in the following screenshot:

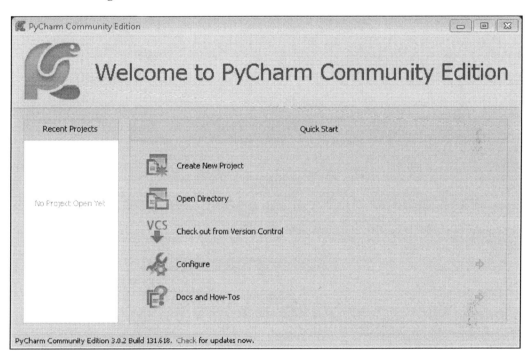

3. On the **Create New Project** dialog box, as shown in next screenshot, specify the name of your project in the **Project name** field. In this example, `setests` is used as the project name. We need to configure the interpreter for the first time. Click on the ⬚ button to set up the interpreter, as shown in the following screenshot:

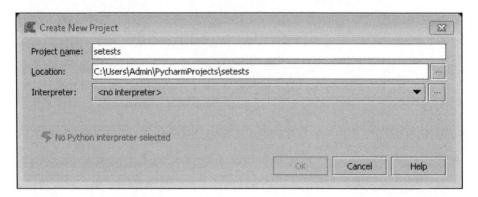

4. On the **Python Interpreter** dialog box, click on the plus icon. PyCharm will suggest the installed interpreter similar to the following screenshot. Select the interpreter from **Select Interpreter Path**.

5. PyCharm will configure the selected interpreter as shown in the following screenshot. It will show a list of packages that are installed along with Python. Click on the **Apply** button and then on the **OK** button:

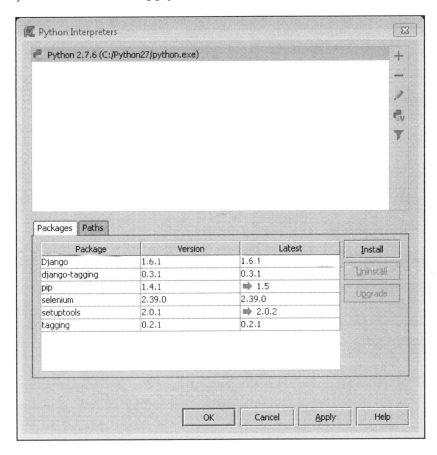

6. On the **Create New Project** dialog box, click on the **OK** button to create the project:

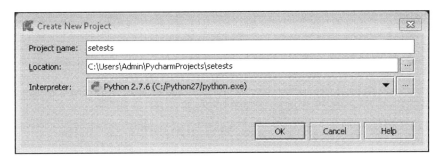

Taking your first steps with Selenium and Python

We are now ready to start with creating and running automated scripts in Python. Let's begin with Selenium WebDriver and create a Python script that uses Selenium WebDriver classes and functions to automate browser interaction.

We will use a sample web application for most of the examples in this book. This sample application is built on a famous e-commerce framework—**Magento**. You can find the application at `http://demo.magentocommerce.com/`.

> **Downloading the example code**
>
> You can download the example code files from your account at `http://www.packtpub.com` for all the Packt Publishing books you have purchased. If you purchased this book elsewhere, you can visit `http://www.packtpub.com/support` and register to have the files e-mailed directly to you.
>
> The example code is also hosted at `https://github.com/upgundecha/learnsewithpython`.

In this sample script, we will navigate to the demo version of the application, search for products, and list the names of products from the search result page with the following steps:

1. Let's use the project that we created earlier while setting up PyCharm. Create a simple Python script that will use the Selenium WebDriver client library. In Project Explorer, right-click on `setests` and navigate to **New | Python File** from the pop-up menu:

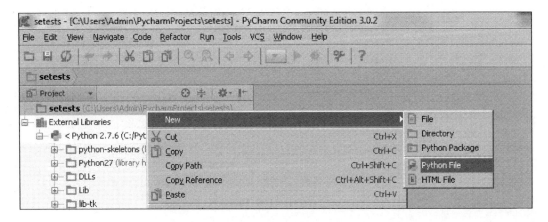

2. On the **New Python file** dialog box, enter `searchproducts` in the **Name** field and click on the **OK** button:

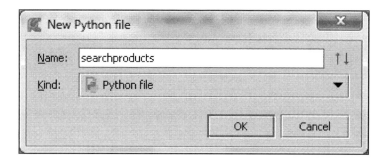

3. PyCharm will add a new tab **searchproducts.py** in the code editor area. Copy the following code in the **searchproduct.py** tab:

```python
from selenium import webdriver

# create a new Firefox session
driver = webdriver.Firefox()
driver.implicitly_wait(30)
driver.maximize_window()

# navigate to the application home page
driver.get("http://demo.magentocommerce.com/")

# get the search textbox
search_field = driver.find_element_by_name("q")
search_field.clear()

# enter search keyword and submit
search_field.send_keys("phones")
search_field.submit()

# get all the anchor elements which have product names displayed
# currently on result page using find_elements_by_xpath method
products = driver.find_elements_by_xpath("//h2[@class='product-name']/a")

# get the number of anchor elements found
print "Found " + str(len(products)) + " products:"

# iterate through each anchor element and print the text that is
# name of the product
for product in products:
    print product.text

# close the browser window
driver.quit()
```

If you're using any other IDE or editor of your choice, create a new file, copy the code to the new file, and save the file as `searchproducts.py`.

4. To run the script, press the *Ctrl + Shift + F10* combination in the PyCharm code window or select **Run 'searchproducts'** from the **Run** menu. This will start the execution and you will see a new Firefox window navigating to the demo site and the Selenium commands getting executed in the Firefox window. If all goes well, at the end, the script will close the Firefox window. The script will print the list of products in the PyCharm console as shown in the following screenshot:

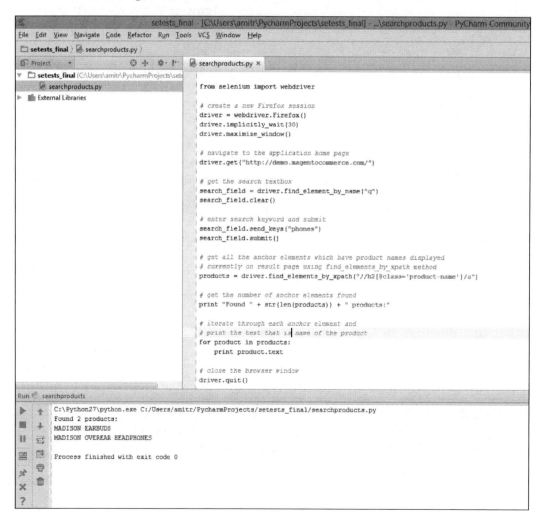

We can also run this script through the command line with the following command. Open the command line, then open the `setests` directory, and run following command:

python searchproducts.py

We will use command line as the preferred method in the rest of the book to execute the tests.

We'll spend some time looking into the script that we created just now. We will go through each statement and understand Selenium WebDriver in brief. There is a lot to go through in the rest of the book.

The `selenium.webdriver` module implements the browser driver classes that are supported by Selenium, including Firefox, Chrome, Internet Explorer, Safari, and various other browsers, and `RemoteWebDriver` to test on browsers that are hosted on remote machines.

We need to import `webdriver` from the Selenium package to use the Selenium WebDriver methods:

```
from selenium import webdriver
```

Next, we need an instance of a browser that we want to use. This will provide a programmatic interface to interact with the browser using the Selenium commands. In this example, we are using Firefox. We can create an instance of Firefox as shown in following code:

```
driver = webdriver.Firefox()
```

During the run, this will launch a new Firefox window. We also set a few options on the driver:

```
driver.implicitly_wait(30)
driver.maximize_window()
```

We configured a timeout for Selenium to execute steps using an implicit wait of 30 seconds for the driver and maximized the Firefox window through the Selenium API. We will learn more about implicit wait in *Chapter 5, Synchronizing Tests*.

Next, we will navigate to the demo version of the application using its URL by calling the `driver.get()` method. After the `get()` method is called, WebDriver waits until the page is fully loaded in the Firefox window and returns the control to the script.

After loading the page, Selenium will interact with various elements on the page, like a human user. For example, on the Home page of the application, we need to enter a search term in a textbox and click on the **Search** button. These elements are implemented as HTML input elements and Selenium needs to find these elements to simulate the user action. Selenium WebDriver provides a number of methods to find these elements and interact with them to perform operations such as sending values, clicking buttons, selecting items in dropdowns, and so on. We will see more about this in *Chapter 3, Finding Elements*.

In this example, we are finding the **Search** textbox using the find_element_by_name method. This will return the first element matching the name attribute specified in the find method. The HTML elements are defined with tag and attributes. We can use this information to find an element, by following the given steps:

1. In this example, the **Search** textbox has the name attribute defined as q and we can use this attribute as shown in the following code example:

    ```
    search_field = driver.find_element_by_name("q")
    ```

2. Once the **Search** textbox is found, we will interact with this element by clearing the previous value (if entered) using the clear() method and enter the specified new value using the send_keys() method. Next, we will submit the search request by calling the submit() method:

    ```
    search_field.clear()
    search_field.send_keys("phones")
    search_field.submit()
    ```

3. After submission of the search request, Firefox will load the result page returned by the application. The result page has a list of products that match the search term, which is phones. We can read the list of results and specifically the names of all the products that are rendered in the anchor <a> element using the find_elements_by_xpath() method. This will return more than one matching element as a list:

    ```
    products =
        driver.find_elements_by_xpath("//h2[@class=
        'product-name']/a")
    ```

4. Next, we will print the number of products (that is the number of anchor <a> elements) that are found on the page and the names of the products using the .text property of all the anchor <a> elements:

    ```
    print "Found " + str(len(products)) + " products:"

    for product in products:
        print product.text
    ```

5. At end of the script, we will close the Firefox browser using the `driver.quit()` method:

```
driver.quit()
```

This example script gives us a concise example of using Selenium WebDriver and Python together to create a simple automation script. We are not testing anything in this script yet. Later in the book, we will extend this simple script into a set of tests and use various other libraries and features of Python.

Cross-browser support

So far we have built and run our script with Firefox. Selenium has extensive support for cross-browser testing where you can automate on all the major browsers including Internet Explorer, Google Chrome, Safari, Opera, and headless browsers such as PhantomJS. In this section, we will set up and run the script that we created in the previous section with Internet Explorer and Google Chrome to see the cross-browser capabilities of Selenium WebDriver.

Setting up Internet Explorer

There is a little more to run scripts on Internet Explorer. To run tests on Internet Explorer, we need to download and set up the `InternetExplorerDriver` server. The `InternetExplorerDriver` server is a standalone server executable that implements WebDriver's wire protocol to work as glue between the test script and Internet Explorer. It supports major IE versions on Windows XP, Vista, Windows 7, and Windows 8 operating systems. Let's set up the `InternetExplorerDriver` server with the following steps:

1. Download the `InternetExplorerDriver` server from `http://www.seleniumhq.org/download/`. You can download 32- or 64-bit versions based on the system configuration that you are using.

2. After downloading the `InternetExplorerDriver` server, unzip and copy the file to the same directory where scripts are stored.

3. On IE 7 or higher, the **Protected Mode** settings for each zone must have the same value. **Protected Mode** can either be on or off, as long as it is for all the zones. To set the **Protected Mode** settings:

   1. Choose **Internet Options** from the **Tools** menu.

   2. On the **Internet Options** dialog box, click on the **Security** tab.

3. Select each zone listed in **Select a zone to view or change security settings** and make sure **Enable Protected Mode (requires restarting Internet Explorer)** is either checked or unchecked for all the zones. All the zones should have the same settings as shown in the following screenshot:

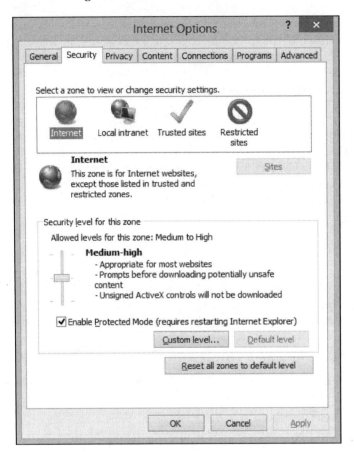

 While using the `InternetExplorerDriver` server, it is also important to keep the browser zoom level set to 100 percent so that the native mouse events can be set to the correct coordinates.

4. Finally, modify the script to use Internet Explorer. Instead of creating an instance of the Firefox class, we will use the `IE` class in the following way:

```
import os
from selenium import webdriver
```

```python
# get the path of IEDriverServer
dir = os.path.dirname(__file__)
ie_driver_path = dir + "\IEDriverServer.exe"

# create a new Internet Explorer session
driver = webdriver.Ie(ie_driver_path)
driver.implicitly_wait(30)
driver.maximize_window()

# navigate to the application home page
driver.get("http://demo.magentocommerce.com/")

# get the search textbox
search_field = driver.find_element_by_name("q")
search_field.clear()

# enter search keyword and submit
search_field.send_keys("phones")
search_field.submit()

# get all the anchor elements which have product names displayed
# currently on result page using find_elements_by_xpath method
products = driver.find_elements_by_xpath("//h2[@class='product-name']/a")

# get the number of anchor elements found
print "Found " + str(len(products)) + " products:"

# iterate through each anchor element and print the text that is
# name of the product
for product in products:
    print product.text

# close the browser window
driver.quit()
```

In this script, we passed the path of the `InternetExplorerDriver` server while creating the instance of an `IE` browser class.

5. Run the script and Selenium will first launch the `InternetExplorerDriver` server, which launches the browser, and execute the steps.

The `InternetExplorerDriver` server acts as an intermediary between the Selenium script and the browser. Execution of the actual steps is very similar to what we observed with Firefox.

Read more about the important configuration options for Internet Explorer at `https://code.google.com/p/selenium/wiki/InternetExplorerDriver` and the *DesiredCapabilities* article at `https://code.google.com/p/selenium/wiki/DesiredCapabilities`.

Setting up Google Chrome

Setting up and running Selenium scripts on Google Chrome is similar to Internet Explorer. We need to download the `ChromeDriver` server similar to `InternetExplorerDriver`. The `ChromeDriver` server is a standalone server developed and maintained by the Chromium team. It implements WebDriver's wire protocol for automating Google Chrome. It is supported on Windows, Linux, and Mac operating systems. Set up the `ChromeDriver` server using the following steps:

1. Download the `ChromeDriver` server from `http://chromedriver.storage.googleapis.com/index.html`.

2. After downloading the `ChromeDriver` server, unzip and copy the file to the same directory where the scripts are stored.

3. Finally, modify the sample script to use Chrome. Instead of creating an instance of the Firefox class, we will use the `Chrome` class in the following way:

    ```python
    import os
    from selenium import webdriver

    # get the path of chromedriver
    dir = os.path.dirname(__file__)
    chrome_driver_path = dir + "\chromedriver.exe"
    #remove the .exe extension on linux or mac platform

    # create a new Chrome session
    driver = webdriver.Chrome(chrome_driver_path)
    driver.implicitly_wait(30)
    driver.maximize_window()

    # navigate to the application home page
    driver.get("http://demo.magentocommerce.com/")

    # get the search textbox
    search_field = driver.find_element_by_name("q")
    search_field.clear()

    # enter search keyword and submit
    ```

```
search_field.send_keys("phones")
search_field.submit()

# get all the anchor elements which have product names displayed
# currently on result page using find_elements_by_xpath method
products = driver.find_elements_by_xpath("//h2[@class='product-
name']/a")

# get the number of anchor elements found
print "Found " + str(len(products)) + " products:"

# iterate through each anchor element and print the text that is
# name of the product
for product in products:
    print product.text

# close the browser window
driver.quit()
```

In this script, we passed the path of the `ChromeDriver` server while creating an instance of the Chrome browser class.

4. Run the script. Selenium will first launch the `Chromedriver` server, which launches the Chrome browser, and execute the steps. Execution of the actual steps is very similar to what we observed with Firefox.

 Read more about ChromeDriver at `https://code.google.com/p/selenium/wiki/ChromeDriver` and `https://sites.google.com/a/chromium.org/chromedriver/home`.

Summary

In this chapter, we introduced you to Selenium and its components. We installed the `selenium` package using the `pip` tool. Then we looked at various Editors and IDEs to ease our coding experience with Selenium and Python and set up PyCharm. Then we built a simple script on a sample application covering some of the high-level concepts of Selenium WebDriver Python client library using Firefox. We ran the script and analyzed the outcome. Finally, we explored the cross-browser testing support of Selenium WebDriver by configuring and running the script with Internet Explorer and Google Chrome.

In next chapter, we will learn how to use the `unittest` library to create automated tests using Selenium WebDriver. We will also learn how to create a suite of tests and run tests in groups.

2

Writing Tests Using unittest

Selenium WebDriver is a browser automation API. It provides features to automate browser interaction, and this API is mainly used to test web applications. We cannot set up test preconditions and post conditions, check the expected and actual output, check the state of the application, report test results, create data-driven tests, and so on with Selenium WebDriver. We can use a unit testing framework or test runners used for unit testing along with Selenium to create a testing framework. In this chapter, we will learn how to use the `unittest` library to create Selenium WebDriver tests in Python.

In this chapter, we will cover the following topics:

- What `unittest` is?
- Using the `unittest` library to write Selenium WebDriver tests
- Implementing a test using the `TestCase` class
- Understanding various types of `assert` methods provided by the `unittest` library
- Creating a `TestSuite` for a group of tests
- Generating test reports in HTML format using the `unittest` extension

The unittest library

The `unittest` library (originally named as PyUnit) is inspired by the JUnit library widely used in Java application development. We can use `unittest` to create a comprehensive suite of tests for any project. The `unittest` module is used within the Python project to test various standard library modules including `unittest` itself. You can find the `unittest` documentation at `http://docs.python.org/2/library/unittest.html`.

The `unittest` library provides us with the ability to create test cases, test suites, and test fixtures. Let's understand each of these components as shown in following diagram:

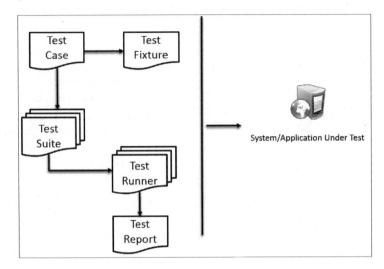

- **Test Fixture**: By using a test fixture, we can define the preparation needed to perform one or more tests and any associated clean-up actions.

- **Test Case**: A test case is the smallest unit of testing in `unittest`. It checks for a specific response to a particular set of actions and inputs using various `assert` methods provided by the `unittest` library. The `unittest` library provides a base class called `TestCase` that may be used to create new test cases.

- **Test Suite**: A test suite is a collection of multiple tests or test cases to create groups of tests representing specific functionality or modules of the application under test, which will be executed together.

- **Test Runner**: The test runner orchestrates execution of tests and provides results to the user. The runner may use a graphical interface, a textual interface, or return a special value to indicate the results of executing the tests.

- **Test Report**: A test report displays a summary of test results showing the pass or fail status of executed test cases, expected versus actual results for failed steps, and summary of overall run and timing information.

A test created with the `xUnit` framework such as `unittest` is divided into three parts also known as the 3 A's, as follows:

- **Arrange**: This part sets up the preconditions for tests including the object(s) that need to be tested, related configuration, and dependencies

- **Act**: This part exercises the functionality
- **Assert**: This part checks the outcome with the expected results

We will use this approach to create tests with the `unittest` library in rest of the chapter.

> We will use the `unittest` library in rest of the book to create and run Selenium WebDriver tests. However, there are other testing frameworks available in Python with additional features, as follows:
>
> - **Nose**: The `nose` framework extends the `unittest` library and provides ability to search and run tests automatically. It also provides various plugins to create more advanced tests. You can find more about nose at `https://nose.readthedocs.org/en/latest/`.
> - **Pytest**: The `pytest` framework is another testing framework that offers a number of advanced features to write and run unit tests in Python. You can find out more about `pytest` at `http://pytest.org/latest/`.

The TestCase class

We can create a test, or group of tests, by inheriting the `TestCase` class and adding each test as a method to this class. To make a test, we need to either use `assert` or one of the many variations on `assert` that are part of the `TestCase` class. The most important task of each test is a call to `assertEqual()` to check for an expected result, `assertTrue()` to verify a condition, or `assertRaises()` to verify that an expected exception gets raised.

In addition to adding tests, we can add test fixtures: that is the `setUp()` and `tearDown()` methods to handle creation and disposition of any objects or conditions that are needed for a test.

Let's start using the `unittest` library, first writing a simple test by inheriting the `TestCase` class and then adding a test method for the sample script that we created in *Chapter 1, Getting Started with Selenium WebDriver and Python*.

We need to import the `unittest` module and define a class that inherits the `TestCase` class, as shown here:

```
import unittest
from selenium import webdriver

class SearchTest(unittest.TestCase):
```

The setUp() method

The starting point for test cases is the `setUp()` method, which we can use to perform some tasks at the start of each test or all the tests that will be defined in the class. These can be test preparation tasks such as creating an instance of a browser driver, navigating to the base URL, loading test data, opening logfiles, and so on.

This method takes no arguments and doesn't return anything. When a `setUp()` method is defined, the test runner will run that method prior to each test method. In our example, we will use the `setUp()` method to create an instance of Firefox, set up the properties, and navigate to the main page of the application before a test is executed as shown in the following example:

```
import unittest
from selenium import webdriver

class SearchTests(unittest.TestCase):
    def setUp(self):
        # create a new Firefox session
        self.driver = webdriver.Firefox()
        self.driver.implicitly_wait(30)
        self.driver.maximize_window()

        # navigate to the application home page
        self.driver.get("http://demo.magentocommerce.com/")
```

Writing tests

With a setup method in place, we can now write some tests to verify the application's functionality that we want to test. In this example, we will search for a product and check if the result returns a number of items. Similar to the `setUp()` method, test methods are implemented in the `TestCase` class. It is important that we name these methods beginning with the word `test`. This naming convention informs the test runner about which methods represent a test.

For each test method that the test runner finds, it executes the `setUp()` method before executing the `test` method. This helps ensure that each `test` method can depend on a consistent environment, regardless of how many tests are defined in the class. We will use a simple `assertEqual()` method to check that the expected results for the given search term match with the results returned by the application. We will discuss more about assertions later in the chapter.

Add a new test method, `test_search_by_category()`, which searches for products by category and checks for the number of products returned by the search, as shown in following example:

```python
import unittest
from selenium import webdriver

class SearchTests(unittest.TestCase):
    def setUp(self):
        # create a new Firefox session
        self.driver = webdriver.Firefox()
        self.driver.implicitly_wait(30)
        self.driver.maximize_window()

        # navigate to the application home page
        self.driver.get("http://demo.magentocommerce.com/")

    def test_search_by_category(self):
        # get the search textbox
        self.search_field = self.driver.find_element_by_name("q")
        self.search_field.clear()

        # enter search keyword and submit
        self.search_field.send_keys("phones")
        self.search_field.submit()

        # get all the anchor elements which have product names
        # displayed currently on result page using
        # find_elements_by_xpath method
        products = self.driver.find_elements_by_xpath
          ("//h2[@class='product-name']/a")
        self.assertEqual(2, len(products))
```

Cleaning up the code

Similar to the `setUp()` method that is called before each test method, the `TestCase` class also calls a `tearDown()` method to clean up any initialized values after the test is executed. Once a test is executed, the values defined in the `setUp()` method are no longer required; so, it is good practice to clean up the values initialized by the `setUp()` method after a test is completed. In our example, after a test is executed, we no longer need the instance of Firefox. We will close the Firefox instance that was created for the test in the `tearDown()` method, as shown in the following code:

```python
import unittest
from selenium import webdriver

class SearchTests(unittest.TestCase):
```

```
    def setUp(self):
        # create a new Firefox session
        self.driver = webdriver.Firefox()
        self.driver.implicitly_wait(30)
        self.driver.maximize_window()

        # navigate to the application home page
        self.driver.get("http://demo.magentocommerce.com/")

    def test_search_by_category(self):
        # get the search textbox
        self.search_field = self.driver.find_element_by_name("q")
        self.search_field.clear()

        # enter search keyword and submit
        self.search_field.send_keys("phones")
        self.search_field.submit()

        # get all the anchor elements which have product names
        # displayed currently on result page using
        # find_elements_by_xpath method
        products = self.driver.find_elements_by_xpath
            ("//h2[@class='product-name']/a")
        self.assertEqual(2, len(products))

    def tearDown(self):
        # close the browser window
        self.driver.quit()
```

Running the test

To run the test from command line, we can add a call to the main method of the test case. We will pass the verbosity argument that is used to display the amount of test result details on the console:

```
if __name__ == '__main__':
    unittest.main(verbosity=2)
```

We can store the tests as a normal Python script. For this example, save the sample test as searchtests.py. After saving the file, we can execute it through command line by using the following command:

```
python searchtests.py
```

After running the tests, `unittest` shows the results on the console along with the summary of tests as shown in the following screenshot:

```
C:\Windows\system32\cmd.exe                                    _ □ ✕

C:\setests\chapter2>searchtests.py
test_search_by_category (__main__.SearchTests) ... ok

----------------------------------------------------------------------
Ran 1 test in 28.354s

OK
```

In addition to the results summary, when a test case fails, for each failure, summary will produce a block of text to describe what went wrong. Look at the following screenshot to see what happens when we change the expected value to something else:

```
C:\Windows\system32\cmd.exe                                    _ □ ✕

C:\setests\chapter2>searchtests.py
test_search_by_category (__main__.SearchTests) ... FAIL

======================================================================
FAIL: test_search_by_category (__main__.SearchTests)
----------------------------------------------------------------------
Traceback (most recent call last):
  File "C:\setests\chapter2\searchtests.py", line 26, in test_search_by_category
    self.assertEqual(len(products), 4)
AssertionError: 3 != 4

----------------------------------------------------------------------
Ran 1 test in 28.718s

FAILED (failures=1)
```

As you can see, it shows exactly which test method generated the failure, with trace-back information to track down the code flow that led to the failure. In addition, the failure itself is shown as `AssertionError`, with a mismatch of the expected output with the actual output.

Adding another test

We can group a number of tests as part of one test class. This helps in creating logical groups of tests that belong to a specific functionality. Let's add another test to the test class. The rule is simple; name the new method starting with the word test, as shown in the following code:

```
def test_search_by_name(self):
    # get the search textbox
    self.search_field = self.driver.find_element_by_name("q")
    self.search_field.clear()

    # enter search keyword and submit
    self.search_field.send_keys("salt shaker")
    self.search_field.submit()

    # get all the anchor elements which have
    # product names displayed
    # currently on result page using
    # find_elements_by_xpath method
    products = self.driver.find_elements_by_xpath
        ("//h2[@class='product-name']/a")
    self.assertEqual(1, len(products))
```

Run the test and you will see two instances of Firefox opening and closing. This is how the setUp() and tearDown() methods work for each test method. You will see the result as shown in the following screenshot:

```
C:\Windows\system32\cmd.exe

C:\setests\chapter2>searchtests.py
test_search_by_category (__main__.SearchTests) ... ok
test_search_by_name (__main__.SearchTests) ... ok

----------------------------------------------------------------------
Ran 2 tests in 61.746s

OK
```

Class-level setUp() and tearDown() methods

In the previous example, we created a new instance of Firefox using the `setUp()` method before the execution of each test method and closed that instance after the execution of the test method. How about sharing a single Firefox instance between the methods instead of creating a new instance every time? This can be done by using the `setUpClass()` and `tearDownClass()` methods and using the `@classmethod` decorator. These methods allow us to initialize values at the class level instead of the method level and then share these values between the test methods. In the following example, the code is modified to call the `setUpClass()` and `tearDownClass()` methods with the `@classmethod` decorator:

```python
import unittest
from selenium import webdriver

class SearchTests(unittest.TestCase):
    @classmethod
    def setUpClass(cls):
        # create a new Firefox session
        cls.driver = webdriver.Firefox()
        cls.driver.implicitly_wait(30)
        cls.driver.maximize_window()

        # navigate to the application home page
        cls.driver.get("http://demo.magentocommerce.com/")
        cls.driver.title

    def test_search_by_category(self):
        # get the search textbox
        self.search_field = self.driver.find_element_by_name("q")
        self.search_field.clear()

        # enter search keyword and submit
        self.search_field.send_keys("phones")
        self.search_field.submit()

        # get all the anchor elements which have product names
        # displayed currently on result page using
        # find_elements_by_xpath method
        products = self.driver.find_elements_by_xpath
          ("//h2[@class='product-name']/a")
        self.assertEqual(2, len(products))
```

```python
    def test_search_by_name(self):
        # get the search textbox
        self.search_field = self.driver.find_element_by_name("q")
        self.search_field.clear()

        # enter search keyword and submit
        self.search_field.send_keys("salt shaker")
        self.search_field.submit()

        # get all the anchor elements which have product names
        # displayed currently on result page using
        # find_elements_by_xpath method
        products = self.driver.find_elements_by_xpath
            ("//h2[@class='product-name']/a")
        self.assertEqual(1, len(products))

    @classmethod
    def tearDownClass(cls):
        # close the browser window
        cls.driver.quit()

if __name__ == '__main__':
    unittest.main()
```

Run the test and you will see a single Firefox instance created; both the tests will use this instance.

> For more information on the @classmethod decorator,
> refer to https://docs.python.org/2/library/
> functions.html#classmethod.

Assertions

The TestCase class of the unittest library offers a number of utility methods to check the expected values against actual values returned by the application. These methods are implemented in such a way that they represent a condition that must be true in order to continue the execution of the test. There are broadly three types of such methods, each covering a specific type of condition such as checking equivalence, logical comparison, and exceptions. If the given assertion passes, the test will continue to the next line of code; otherwise, the test halts immediately and a failure message will be generated.

The `unittest` library provides all the standard xUnit `asserts` methods. The following table lists some of the important methods that we will be using in the rest of the book:

Method	Condition that is checked	Example uses
`assertEqual(a, b [,msg])`	a == b	These methods check whether or not a and b are equal to each other. The `msg` object is a message explaining the failure (if any).
`assertNotEqual(a, b[,msg])`	a != b	
		This is useful to check values of elements, attributes, and so on. For example:
		`assertEqual(element.text,"10")`
`assertTrue(x[,msg]))`	bool(x) is True	These methods check whether the given expression evaluates to `True` or `False`.
`assertFalse(x[,msg]))`	bool(x) is False	For example, to check whether the element is displayed on a page, we can use the following method:
`assertIsNot(a, b[,msg]))`	a is not b	`assertTrue(element.is_dispalyed())`
`assertRaises(exc, fun, *args, **kwds)`	fun(*args, **kwds) raises exc	These methods check whether the specific exceptions are raised by the test steps. A possible use of this method is to check `NoSuchElementFoundexception`.
`assertRaisesRegexp(exc, r, fun, *args, **kwds)`	fun(*args, **kwds) raises exc and the message matches regex r	
`assertAlmostEqual(a, b)`	round(a-b, 7) == 0	These methods specifically check for numeric values, and round the value to the given number of decimal places before checking for equality. This helps account for rounding errors and other problems due to floating-point arithmetic.
`assertNotAlmostEqual(a, b)`	round(a-b, 7) != 0	
`assertGreater(a, b)`	a > b	These methods are similar to the `assertEqual()` method, designed with logical conditions.
`assertGreaterEqual(a, b)`	a >= b	
`assertLess(a, b)`	a < b	
`assertLessEqual(a, b)`	a <= b	

Method	Condition that is checked	Example uses
`assertRegexpMatches(s, r)`	r.search(s)	These methods check whether a `regexp` search matches the text.
`assertNotRegexpMatches(s, r)`	not r.search(s)	
`assertMultiLineEqual(a, b)`	strings	This method is a specialized form of `assertEqual()`, designed for multiline strings. Equality works like any other string, but the default failure message is optimized to show the differences between the values.
`assertListEqual(a, b)`	lists	This method checks whether the lists a and b match. This is useful to match options from drop-down fields.
`fail()`		This method fails the test unconditionally. This can also be used to create custom conditional blocks where other `assert` methods do not work easily.

Test suites

Using the `TestSuites` feature of `unittest`, we can collect various tests into logical groups and then into a unified test suite that can be run with a single command. This is done by using the `TestSuite`, `TestLoader`, and `TestRunner` classes.

Before we get into details of `TestSuite`, let's add a new test to check the home page of the sample application. We will aggregate this test along with the previous search tests into a single test suite, as shown in the following code:

```
import unittest
from selenium import webdriver
from selenium.common.exceptions import NoSuchElementException
from selenium.webdriver.common.by import By
from __builtin__ import classmethod

class HomePageTest(unittest.TestCase):
    @classmethod
    def setUp(cls):
        # create a new Firefox session """
        cls.driver = webdriver.Firefox()
        cls.driver.implicitly_wait(30)
        cls.driver.maximize_window()
```

```
    # navigate to the application home page """
    cls.driver.get("http://demo.magentocommerce.com/")

def test_search_field(self):
    # check search field exists on Home page
    self.assertTrue(self.is_element_present(By.NAME,"q"))

def test_language_option(self):
    # check language options dropdown on Home page
    self.assertTrue(self.is_element_present
      (By.ID,"select-language"))

def test_shopping_cart_empty_message(self):
    # check content of My Shopping Cart block on Home page
    shopping_cart_icon = \
        self.driver.find_element_by_css_selector
          ("div.header-minicart span.icon")
    shopping_cart_icon.click()

    shopping_cart_status = \
        self.driver.find_element_by_css_selector
          ("p.empty").text
    self.assertEqual("You have no items in your shopping cart.",
    shopping_cart_status)

    close_button =  self.driver.find_element_by_css_selector
      ("div.minicart-wrapper a.close")
    close_button.click()

@classmethod
def tearDown(cls):
    # close the browser window
    cls.driver.quit()


def is_element_present(self, how, what):
    """
    Utility method to check presence of an element on page
    :params how: By locator type
    :params what: locator value
    """
    try: self.driver.find_element(by=how, value=what)
    except NoSuchElementException, e: return False
    return True

if __name__ == '__main__':
    unittest.main(verbosity=2)
```

We will use the `TestSuite` class for defining and running the test suite. We can add multiple test cases to the test suite. In addition to the `TestSuite` class we need to use `TestLoader` and `TextTestRunner` to create and run a test suite as shown in the following code:

```
import unittest
from searchtests import SearchTests
from homepagetests import HomePageTest

# get all tests from SearchProductTest and HomePageTest class
search_tests = unittest.TestLoader().loadTestsFromTestCase
(SearchTests)
home_page_tests = unittest.TestLoader().loadTestsFromTestCase
(HomePageTest)

# create a test suite combining search_test and home_page_test
smoke_tests = unittest.TestSuite([home_page_tests, search_tests])

# run the suite
unittest.TextTestRunner(verbosity=2).run(smoke_tests)
```

Using the `TestLoader` class, we will get all the test methods from the specified test files that will be used to create the test suite. The `TestRunner` class will take the test suite and run all the tests from these files.

We can run the new test suite file using the following command:

python smoketests.py

This will run all the tests from the `SearchProductTest` and `HomePageTest` class and generate the following output in the console:

Generating the HTML test report

The unittest library generates the test output on a console window. You might want to generate a report of all the tests executed as evidence or to distribute test results to various stakeholders. Sending console logs to the stakeholder may not be a good idea. Stakeholders will need nicely formatted, summary reports with a drill-down access to the details. The unittest library does not have an in-built way to generate nicely formatted reports. We can use the HTMLTestRunner extension of unittest written by Wai Yip Tung. You can find more about HTMLTestRunner at https://pypi.python.org/pypi/HTMLTestRunner along with the download instructions.

 The HTMLTestRunner extension is bundled with the book's source code.

We will use HTMLTestRunner in our test to generate a nice-looking report. Let's modify the test suite file that we created earlier in the chapter and add HTMLTestRunner support. We need to create an output file that will contain the actual report, configure the HTMLTestRunner options, and run the tests in the following way:

```
import unittest
import HTMLTestRunner
import os
from searchtests import SearchTests
from homepagetests import HomePageTest

# get the directory path to output report file
dir = os.getcwd()

# get all tests from SearchProductTest and HomePageTest class
search_tests = unittest.TestLoader().loadTestsFromTestCase(SearchTes
ts)
home_page_tests = unittest.TestLoader().loadTestsFromTestCase(HomePag
eTest)

# create a test suite combining search_test and home_page_test
smoke_tests = unittest.TestSuite([home_page_tests, search_tests])

# open the report file
outfile = open(dir + "\SmokeTestReport.html", "w")

# configure HTMLTestRunner options
runner = HTMLTestRunner.HTMLTestRunner(
                stream=outfile,
                title='Test Report',
                description='Smoke Tests'
                )
```

```
# run the suite using HTMLTestRunner
runner.run(smoke_tests)
```

Run the test suite; HTMLTestRunner executes all the tests similar to the unittest library's default test runner. At the end of the execution, it will generate a report file as shown in the following screenshot:

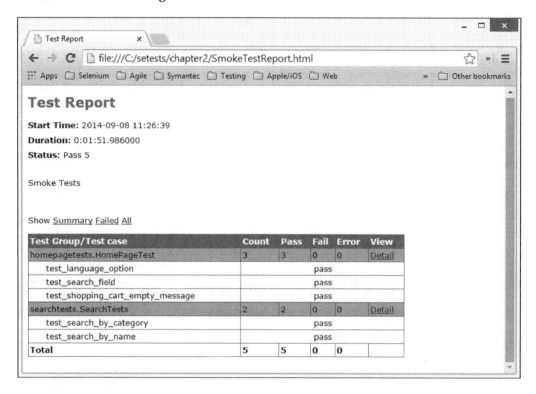

Summary

In this chapter, we learned how to use the unittest testing library for writing and running tests with Selenium WebDriver. We created a test using the TestClass class with the setUp() and tearDown() methods. We added an assertion to check the expected output with the actual output.

We also learned how to use different types of assertions that are supported by the unittest library. We implemented the test suite that provides the ability to aggregate tests in logical groups. Finally, we used HTMLTestRunner to generate test reports in HTML format that show nicely formatted test results.

In the next chapter, we will learn how to use and define locators to interact with various HTML elements displayed on a page.

3
Finding Elements

Web applications and the web pages within these applications are written in a mixture of the **Hyper Text Markup Language** (**HTML**), **Cascading Style Sheets** (**CSS**), and JavaScript code. Based on user actions such as navigating to a website **Uniform Resource Locator** (**URL**) or clicking on a submit button, a browser sends a request to a web server. The web server processes this request and sends the response with HTML and related resources such as JavaScript, CSS, and images, and so on back to the browser. The information received from the server is used by the browser to render a web page with various visual elements such as textboxes, buttons, labels, tables, forms, checkboxes, radio boxes, lists, images, and so on, on the page. While doing so, the browser hides the HTML code and related resources from the user. The user is presented with a graphical user interface in the browser window. The various visual elements or controls used on pages are known as **WebElements** in Selenium.

In this chapter, we will cover the following topics:

- Understanding more about finding elements with Selenium WebDriver
- Understanding how to investigate and define locators to find elements using developer tools options available in various browsers
- Finding out various ways to find elements, including `ID`, `Name`, and `Class` attribute values and use XPath and CSS selectors to define more dynamic locators
- Implementing various `find_element_by` methods to find elements so that we can automate interaction on these elements using Selenium WebDriver

When we want to automate browser interaction using Selenium, we need to tell Selenium how to find a particular element or set of elements on a web page programmatically and simulate user actions on these elements. Selenium provides various selector or locator methods to find elements based on their attribute/value criteria or selector value that we supply in script.

How do we find the selector or locator information? Web pages are written in a mixture of HTML, CSS, and JavaScript. We can derive this information by looking at the HTML source of the page. We need to find information such as what HTML tag is used for the element that we want to interact with, the defined attribute, and the values for the attributes and the structure of the page. Let's take a look at a sample form in the application we're testing. Here is an example of the search field and the search (the magnifying glass) icon from the sample application in the following screenshot:

Let's look at the HTML code written for the search form:

```
<form id="search_mini_form" action=
  "http://demo.magentocommerce.com/catalogsearch/result/"
  method="get">
    <div class="form-search">
        <label for="search">Search:</label>
        <input id="search" type="text" name="q" value=""
          class="input-text" maxlength="128" />
        <button type="submit" title="Search"
          class="button"><span><span>Search</span></span></button>
        <div id="search_autocomplete" class="search-
          autocomplete"></div>
        <script type="text/javascript">
        //<![CDATA[
            var searchForm = new Varien.searchForm
              ('search_mini_form', 'search', 'Search entire store
              here...');
            searchForm.initAutocomplete
              ('http://demo.magentocommerce.com
              /catalogsearch/ajax/suggest/',
              'search_autocomplete');
        //]]>
        </script>
    </div>
</form>
```

Each element such as the search textbox and search button is implemented using an `<input>` tag inside a `<form>` tag and labels are implemented using the `<label>` tag. There is some JavaScript code written in the `<script>` tag.

The search textbox that is represented as the `<input>` tag has `id`, `type`, `name`, `value`, `class`, and `maxlength` attributes defined:

```
<input id="search" type="text" name="q" value=""
  class="input-text" maxlength="128" />
```

We can view code written for a page by right-clicking on the browser window and selecting the **View Page Source** option from the pop-up menu. It will display HTML and client-side JavaScript code for the page in a separate window.

 If you're new to HTML, CSS, and JavaScript, then it's worth looking at some useful tutorials at `http://www.w3schools.com/`. These will help you in identifying locators using different ways supported by Selenium WebDriver.

Using developer tools to find locators

While writing Selenium tests, we will often need to look at the web page code and might need special tools that can display information in a structured and easy-to-understand format. Good news, the majority of the browsers have built-in features or add-ons to help us. These tools provide us with a neat and clean way to understand how elements and their attributes are defined on a page, DOM structure, JavaScript blocks, CSS style attributes, and so on. Let's explore these tools in more detail and see how we can use them.

Inspecting pages and elements with Firefox using the Firebug add-in

Newer versions of Firefox provide built-in ways to analyze the page and elements; however, we will use the Firebug add-in, which has more powerful features, by following the given steps:

1. You need to download and install the Firebug add-in in Firefox available at `https://addons.mozilla.org/en-us/firefox/addon/firebug/`.

2. To inspect the page using Firebug, move the mouse over a desired element and right-click to open the pop-up menu.

3. Select the **Inspect Element with Firebug** option from the pop-up menu.

    This will display the Firebug section along with all the information about the page and the selected element including HTML code in a tree format as shown in the following screenshot:

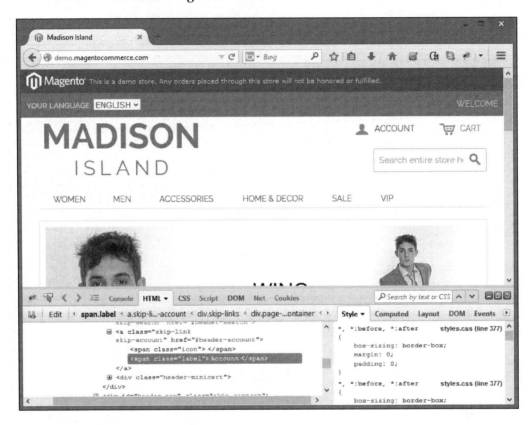

4. Using Firebug, we can also validate XPath or CSS selectors using the search box shown in the Firebug section. Just enter the XPath or CSS selector, and Firebug will highlight the element(s) that match the expression, as shown in the following screenshot:

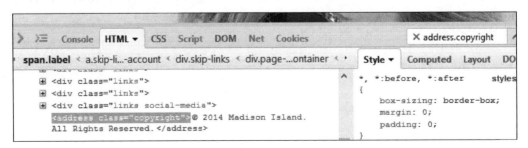

Inspecting pages and elements with Google Chrome

Google Chrome provides a built-in feature to analyze an element or page. You can inspect pages and elements by following the given steps:

1. Move the mouse over a desired element on a page and right-click to open the pop-up menu; then select the **Inspect element** option.

   This will open the developer tools in the browser, which display information similar to that of Firebug, as shown in the following screenshot:

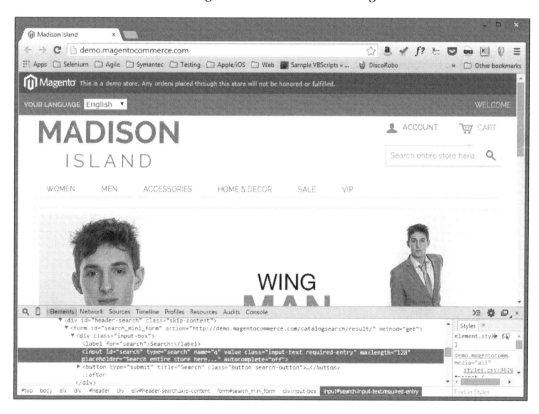

2. Similar to Firebug in Firefox, we can also test XPath and CSS selectors in the Google Chrome Developer Tools. Press *Ctrl + F* in the **Elements** tab. This will display a search box. Just enter the XPath or CSS selector and Firebug will highlight element(s) that match the expression, as shown in the following screenshot:

Inspecting pages and elements with Internet Explorer

Microsoft Internet Explorer also provides built-in features to analyze elements or pages. You can inspect pages and elements by following the given steps:

1. To open the developer tools, press the *F12* key. The developer tools section will be displayed at the bottom of browser.

2. To inspect an element, click on the pointer icon and hover over the desired element on the page. The developer tools will highlight the element with a blue outline and display the HTML code in a tree as shown in the following screenshot:

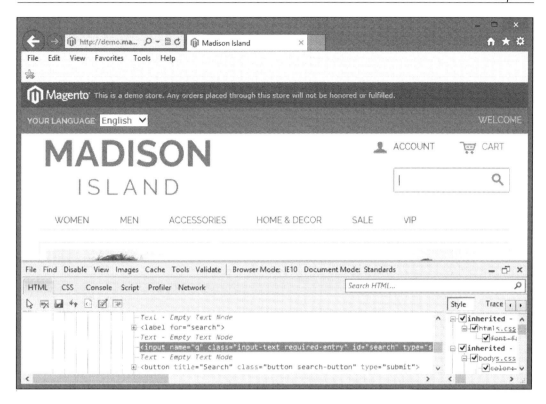

You will find these tools very useful while writing tests. Some of these tools also provide the ability to run JavaScript code for debugging and testing.

Finding elements with Selenium WebDriver

We need to tell Selenium how to find an element so that it can simulate a desired user action, or look at the attributes or state of an element so that we can perform a check. For example, if we want to search for a product, we need to find the search text field and search button visually. We enter the search term by pressing various keys on the keyboard and click on the search button to submit our search request.

We can automate the same actions using Selenium. However, Selenium does not understand these fields or buttons visually as we do. It needs to find the search textbox and search button to simulate keyboard entry and mouse click programmatically.

Selenium provides various `find_element_by` methods to find elements on a web page. These methods search for an element based on the criteria supplied to them. If a matching element is found, an instance of WebElement is returned or the `NoSuchElementException` exception is thrown if Selenium is not able to find any element matching the search criteria.

Selenium also provides various `find_elements_by` methods to locate multiple elements. These methods search and return a list of elements that match the supplied values.

Using the find methods

Selenium provides eight `find_element_by` methods to locate elements. In this section, we will see each one of them in detail. The following table lists `find_element_by` methods:

Method	Description	Argument	Example
`find_element_by_id(id)`	This method finds an element by the ID attribute value	id: The ID of the element to be found	`driver.find_element_by_id('search')`
`find_element_by_name(name)`	This method finds an element by the name attribute value	name: The name of the element to be found	`driver.find_element_by_name('q')`
`find_element_by_class_name(name)`	This method finds an element by the class attribute value	name: The class name of the element to be found	`driver.find_element_by_class_name('input-text')`
`find_element_by_tag_name(name)`	This method finds an element by its tag name	name: The tag name of the element to be found	`driver.find_element_by_tag_name('input')`

Method	Description	Argument	Example
`find_element_by_xpath(xpath)`	This method finds an element using XPath	xpath: The xpath of the element to be found	`driver.find_element_by_xpath('//form[0]/div[0]/input[0]')`
`find_element_by_css_selector(css_selector)`	This method finds an element by the CSS selector	css_selector: The CSS selector of the element to be found	`driver.find_element_by_css_selector('#search')`
`find_element_by_link_text(link_text)`	This method finds an element by the link text	link_text: The text of the element to be found	`driver.find_element_by_link_text('Log In')`
`find_element_by_partial_link_text(link_text)`	This method finds an element by a partial match of its link text	link_text: The text to match part of the text of the element	`driver.find_element_by_partial_link_text('Log')`

The following table lists the `find_elements_by` methods that return a list of elements matching the specified criteria:

Method	Description	Argument	Example
`find_elements_by_id(id_)`	This method finds multiple elements using the ID	id_: The ID of the elements to be found	`driver.find_element_by_id('product')`
`find_elements_by_name(name)`	This method finds elements using the name	name: The name of the elements to be found	`driver.find_elements_by_name('products')`
`find_elements_by_class_name(name)`	This method finds elements using the class name	name: The class name of the elements to be found	`driver.find_elements_by_class_name('foo')`

Method	Description	Argument	Example
`find_elements_by_tag_name(name)`	This method finds elements using the tag name	`name`: The tag name of the element to be found	`driver.find_elements_by_tag_name('a')`
`find_elements_by_xpath(xpath)`	This method finds multiple elements by XPath	`xpath`: The xpath of the elements to be found	`driver.find_elements_by_xpath("//div[contains(@class, 'lists')]")`
`find_elements_by_css_selector(css_selector)`	This method finds elements using the CSS selector	`css_selector`: The CSS selector of the element to be found	`driver.find_element_by_css_selector('.input-class')`
`find_elements_by_link_text(text)`	This method finds elements using the link text	`text`: The text of the elements to be found	`driver.find_elements_by_link_text('Log In')`
`find_elements_by_partial_link_text(link_text)`	This method finds elements by a partial match of their link text	`link_text`: The text to match part of the text of the elements	`driver.find_element_by_partial_link_text('Add to,')`

Finding elements using the ID attribute

Finding elements using the ID is the most preferable way to find elements on a page. The `find_element_by_id()` and `find_elements_by_id()` methods return an element or a set of elements that have matching ID attribute values.

The `find_element_by_id()` method returns the first element that has a matching ID attribute value. If no element with matching ID attribute is found, a `NoSuchElementException` will be raised.

Let's try finding the search textbox from the sample application as shown in the following screenshot:

Here is the HTML code for the search textbox with an ID attribute value defined as `search`:

```
<input id="search" type="text" name="q" value=""
    class="input-text" maxlength="128" autocomplete="off">
```

Here is a test that uses the `find_element_by_id()` method to find the search textbox and check its `maxlength` attribute. We will pass the ID attribute's value, `search`, to the `find_element_by_id()` method:

```
def test_search_text_field_max_length(self):
    # get the search textbox
    search_field = self.driver.find_element_by_id("search")

    # check maxlength attribute is set to 128
    self.assertEqual("128", search_field.get_attribute("maxlength"))
```

The `find_elements_by_id()` method returns all the elements that have the same ID attribute values.

Finding elements using the name attribute

Finding an element by its name attribute value is another preferred method. The `find_element_by_name()` and `find_elements_by_name()` methods return element(s) that have matching name attribute value. If no element is found with matching name attribute value, a `NoSuchElementException` will be raised.

In the previous example, we can find the search textbox using its name attribute value instead of the ID attribute value in the following way:

```
# get the search textbox
self.search_field = self.driver.find_element_by_name("q")
```

The `find_elements_by_name()` method returns all the elements that have the same name attribute values.

Finding elements using the class name

Apart from using the ID and name attributes, we can also use the class attributes to find elements. The class attribute is used to apply CSS to an element. The `find_element_by_class_name()` and `find_elements_by_class_name()` methods return element(s) that have matching class attribute value. If no element is found with the matching name attribute value, a `NoSuchElementException` will be raised.

> Finding elements using ID, name, or class attributes is the most preferred and fastest way to find elements. Selenium WebDriver also offers a set of methods when these methods are not sufficient to find an element. We will see these methods later in the chapter.

Let's find the search button displayed in the following screenshot using its class attribute value using the `find_element_by_class_name()` method:

The search button (the magnifying glass icon) is implemented using the `<button>` element with type, title, and class attribute values defined as shown in the following HTML code:

```
<button type="submit" title="Search"
  class="button"><span><span>Search</span></span></button>
```

Let's create a test that finds the search button element using its class attribute value and check whether it is enabled as shown in following code:

```
def test_search_button_enabled(self):
    # get Search button
    search_button = self.driver.find_element_by_class_name
      ("button")

    # check Search button is enabled
    self.assertTrue(search_button.is_enabled())
```

The `find_elements_by_class_name()` method returns all the elements that have the identical class name attribute values.

Finding elements using the tag name

The `find_element_by_tag_name()` and `find_elements_by_tag_name()` methods find element(s) by their HTML tag name. These methods are similar to the `getElementsByTagName()` DOM method in JavaScript. If no element is found with a matching tag name, a `NoSuchElementException` will be raised.

These methods are useful when we want to find elements using their tag name. For example, to find all the `<tr>` tags in a table to find the number of rows.

The home page of the sample application displays promotional banner images as shown in the following screenshot:

These banners are implemented using an `<img>` or image tag inside a `<ul>` or unordered list tag as shown in the following HTML code:

```
<ul class="promos">
    <li>
        <a href="http://demo.magentocommerce.com/home-decor.html">
            <img src="/media/wysiwyg/homepage-three-column-promo-
                01B.png" alt="Physical &amp; Virtual Gift Cards">
        </a>
    </li>
    <li>
        <a href="http://demo.magentocommerce.com/vip.html">
            <img src="/media/wysiwyg/homepage-three-column-promo-
                02.png" alt="Shop Private Sales - Members Only">
        </a>
    </li>
    <li>
        <a href="http://demo.magentocommerce.com/accessories/
          bags-luggage.html">
            <img src="/media/wysiwyg/homepage-three-column-
                promo-03.png" alt="Travel Gear for Every Occasion">
        </a>
    </li>
</ul>
```

We will use the `find_elements_by_tag_name()` method to get all the images. In this example, we will first find the list of banners implemented as `<ul>` or unordered lists using the `find_element_by_class_name()` method and then get all the `<img>` or image elements by calling the `find_elements_by_tag_name()` method on the banners list:

```python
def test_count_of_promo_banners_images(self):
    # get promo banner list
    banner_list = self.driver.find_element_by_class_name("promos")

    # get images from the banner_list
    banners = banner_list.find_elements_by_tag_name("img")

    # check there are 20 tags displayed on the page
    self.assertEqual(2, len(banners))
```

Finding elements using XPath

XPath is a query language used to search and locate nodes in an XML document. All the major web browsers support XPath. Selenium can leverage and use powerful XPath queries to find elements on a web page.

One of the advantages of using XPath is when we can't find a suitable ID, name, or class attribute value for the element. We can use XPath to either find the element in absolute terms or relative to an element that does have an ID or name attribute. We can also use defined attributes other than the ID, name, or class with XPath queries. We can also find elements with the help of a partial check on attribute values using XPath functions such as `starts-with()`, `contains()`, and `ends-with()`.

 To know more about XPath, visit `http://www.w3schools.com/Xpath/` and `http://www.zvon.org/comp/r/tut-XPath_1.html`.

You can find more about XPath locators in the book *Selenium Testing Tools Cookbook, Packt Publishing*.

The `find_element_by_xpath()` and `find_elements_by_xpath()` methods return element(s) that are found by the specified XPath query. For example, we can check whether the promo banners displayed on the home page work as intended and we can open the promotion pages using these images as shown in the following screenshot:

Here is how the Shop Private Sales banner is defined as an `<img>` tag. The image does not have the ID, name, or class attributes defined. Also, we cannot use the `find_by_tag_name()` method as there are multiple `<img>` tags defined on the page. However, by looking at the following HTML code, we can get the `<img>` tag using the `alt` attribute:

```
<ul class="promos">
    ...
    <li>
        <a hrcf="http://demo.magentocommerce.com/vip.html">
            <img src="/media/wysiwyg/homepage-three-column-
                promo-02.png" alt="Shop Private Sales -
                Members Only">
        </a>
    </li>
    ...
</ul>
```

Let's create a test that uses the `find_element_by_xpath()` method. We are using a relative XPath query to find this `<img>` tag using its `alt` attribute (this is how we can use ID, name, and class attributes as well as other attributes such as `title`, `type`, `value`, `alt`, and so on within XPath queries):

```
def test_vip_promo(self):
    # get vip promo image
    vip_promo = self.driver.\
        find_element_by_xpath("//img[@alt='Shop Private Sales
            - Members Only']")

    # check vip promo logo is displayed on home page
    self.assertTrue(vip_promo.is_displayed())
    # click on vip promo images to open the page
    vip_promo.click()
    # check page title
    self.assertEqual("VIP",  self.driver.title)
```

The `find_elements_by_xpath()` method returns all the elements that match the XPath query.

Finding elements using CSS selectors

CSS is a style sheet language used by web designers to describe the look and feel of an HTML document. CSS is used to define various style classes that can be applied to elements for formatting. CSS selectors are used to find HTML elements based on their attributes such as ID, classes, types, attributes, or values and much more to apply the defined CSS rules.

Similar to XPath, Selenium can leverage and use CSS selectors to find elements on a web page. To know more about CSS selectors, visit `http://www.w3schools.com/css/css_selectors.asp/` and `http://www.w3.org/TR/CSS2/selector.html`.

The `find_element_by_css_selector()` and `find_elements_by_css_selector()` methods return element(s) that are found by the specified CSS selector.

On the home page of the sample application, we can see the shopping cart icon. When we click on the icon, we can see the shopping cart. When there are no items added to the shopping cart, a message should be displayed saying **You have no items in your shopping cart**, as shown in the following screenshot:

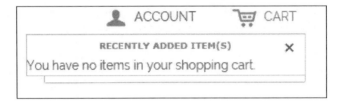

This is implemented as shown in the following HTML code:

```
<div class="minicart-wrapper">
<p class="block-subtitle">
    Recently added item(s)
    <a class="close skip-link-close" href="#" title="Close">
      x</a>
</p>
    <p class="empty">You have no items in your shopping cart.
      </p>
</div>
```

Let's create a test to validate this message. We will use CSS selectors to find the shopping cart icon, click on it, and then find the shopping cart message implemented in the `<p>` or paragraph element:

```
def test_shopping_cart_status(self):
    # check content of My Shopping Cart block on Home page
    # get the Shopping cart icon and click to open the
    # Shopping Cart section
    shopping_cart_icon = self.driver.\
        find_element_by_css_selector("div.header-minicart
            span.icon")
    shopping_cart_icon.click()

    # get the shopping cart status
    shopping_cart_status = self.driver.\
        find_element_by_css_selector("p.empty").text
    self.assertEqual("You have no items in your shopping cart.",
    shopping_cart_status)
    # close the shopping cart section
    close_button = self.driver.\
        find_element_by_css_selector("div.minicart-wrapper
            a.close")
    close_button.click()
```

We used the element tag along with the class name in this example. For example, to get the shopping cart icon, we used the following selector:

```
shopping_cart_icon = self.driver.\
    find_element_by_css_selector("div.header-minicart
        span.icon")
```

This will first find a `<div>` element with the `header_minicart` class name and then find a `<span>` element under this `div`, which has `icon` as its class name.

You can find more about CSS selectors in *Selenium Testing Tools Cookbook*, *Packt Publishing*.

Finding links

The `find_element_by_link_text()` and `find_elements_by_link_text()` methods find link(s) using the text displayed for the link. For example:

1. To get the **Account** link displayed on the Home page, as shown in the following screenshot, we can use the `find_element_by_link_text()` method:

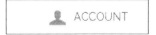

2. Here is the HTML code for the **Account** link implemented as the `<a>` (or anchor tag) and the `<span>` tag with text:

```
<a href="#header-account" class="skip-link skip-account">
  <span class="icon"></span>
  <span class="label">Account</span>
</a>
```

3. Let's create a test that locates the **Account** link using its text and check whether it's displayed:

```
def test_my_account_link_is_displayed(self):
    # get the Account link
    account_link =
      self.driver.find_element_by_link_text("ACCOUNT")

    # check My Account link is displayed/visible in
    # the Home page footer
    self.assertTrue(account_link.is_displayed())
```

The `find_elements_by_link_text()` method gets all the link elements that have matching link text.

Finding links with partial text

The `find_element_by_partial_link_text()` and `find_elements_by_partial_link_text()` methods find link(s) using partial text. These methods are useful where we want to find links using partial text values. Consider the following steps as an example:

1. On the home page of the application, two links are displayed to open the Account page: one in the header section with `Account` as text and the other in the footer with `My Account` as text.

2. Let's use the `find_elements_by_partial_link_text()` method to find these links using the `Account` text and check whether we have two of these links available on the page:

```
def test_account_links(self):
    # get the all the links with Account text in it
    account_links = self.driver.\
        find_elements_by_partial_link_text("ACCOUNT")

    # check Account and My Account link is
      displayed/visible in the Home page footer
    self.assertTrue(2, len(account_links))
```

Putting all the tests together using find methods

In the previous sections, we saw various `find_element_by` methods along with examples. Let's pull together all these examples in a test.

1. Create a new `homepagetest.py` file and copy all the tests that we created earlier as shown in the following code:

```python
import unittest
from selenium import webdriver

class HomePageTest(unittest.TestCase):
    @classmethod
    def setUpClass(cls):
        # create a new Firefox session
        cls.driver = webdriver.Firefox()
        cls.driver.implicitly_wait(30)
        cls.driver.maximize_window()

        # navigate to the application home page
        cls.driver.get('http://demo.magentocommerce.com/')

    def test_search_text_field_max_length(self):
        # get the search textbox
        search_field = self.driver.
          find_element_by_id("search")

        # check maxlength attribute is set to 128
        self.assertEqual("128", search_field.get_attribute
        ("maxlength"))

    def test_search_button_enabled(self):
        # get Search button
        search_button = self.driver.
          find_element_by_class_name("button")

        # check Search button is enabled
        self.assertTrue(search_button.is_enabled())

    def test_my_account_link_is_displayed(self):
        # get the Account link
```

```python
        account_link = \
          self.driver.find_element_by_link_text("ACCOUNT")

        # check My Account link is displayed/visible in
        # the Home page footer
        self.assertTrue(account_link.is_displayed())

    def test_account_links(self):
        # get the all the links with Account text in it
        account_links = self.driver.\
            find_elements_by_partial_link_text("ACCOUNT")

        # check Account and My Account link is
        # displayed/visible in the Home page footer
        self.assertTrue(2, len(account_links))

    def test_count_of_promo_banners_images(self):
        # get promo banner list
        banner_list = self.driver.\
          find_element_by_class_name("promos")

        # get images from the banner_list
        banners = banner_list.\
          find_elements_by_tag_name("img")

        # check there are 3 banners displayed on the page
        self.assertEqual(2, len(banners))

    def test_vip_promo(self):
        # get vip promo image
        vip_promo = self.driver.\
            find_element_by_xpath("//img[@alt=
            'Shop Private Sales - Members Only']")

        # check vip promo logo is displayed on home page
        self.assertTrue(vip_promo.is_displayed())
        # click on vip promo images to open the page
        vip_promo.click()
        # check page title
        self.assertEqual("VIP", self.driver.title)

    def test_shopping_cart_status(self):
        # check content of My Shopping Cart block
        # on Home page
```

```
        # get the Shopping cart icon and click to
        # open the Shopping Cart section
        shopping_cart_icon = self.driver.\
            find_element_by_css_selector("div.header-
                minicart span.icon")
        shopping_cart_icon.click()

        # get the shopping cart status
        shopping_cart_status = self.driver.\
            find_element_by_css_selector("p.empty").text
        self.assertEqual("You have no items in your shopping
        cart.", shopping_cart_status)
        # close the shopping cart section
        close_button = self.driver.\
            find_element_by_css_selector("div.minicart-
            wrapper a.close")
        close_button.click()

    @classmethod
    def tearDownClass(cls):
        # close the browser window
        cls.driver.quit()

if __name__ == '__main__':
    unittest.main(verbosity=2)
```

2. Let's execute all the tests through the command line using the following command:

   ```
   python homepagetest.py
   ```

3. After running the tests, `unittest` shows that seven tests were run and all passed with OK status as shown in the following screenshot:

Summary

In this chapter, you learned one of the most important features of Selenium for finding elements on web pages to simulate user actions.

We looked at various `find_element_by_` methods to find an element using ID, name, class name attributes, tags names, XPath, CSS selectors, and to find links using link text and partial link text.

We implemented tests using various `find_element_by` methods to understand various strategies that we can use to find elements.

This chapter will be the foundation for the coming chapters that delve into using the Selenium API for user interactions.

In the next chapter, you will learn how to use Selenium WebDriver functions to interact with various HTML elements and perform actions such as entering a value in a textbox, clicking on a button, selecting drop-down options, handling JavaScript alerts, and working with frames and windows.

4

Using the Selenium Python API for Element Interaction

Web applications use HTML forms to send data to a server. HTML forms contain input elements such as text fields, checkboxes, radio buttons, submit buttons, and more. A form can also contain select lists, text areas, field sets, legends, and label elements.

A typical web application requires you to fill in lots of forms, starting from registering as a user or searching for products. Forms are enclosed in the HTML `<form>` tag. This tag specifies the method of submitting the data, either using the GET or POST method, and the address at which the data entered into the form should be submitted on the server.

In this chapter, we will cover the following topics:

- Understanding more about the `WebDriver` and `WebElement` classes
- Implementing tests that interact with the application using various methods and properties of the `WebDriver` and `WebElement` classes
- Using the `Select` class to automate dropdowns and lists
- Automating JavaScript alerts and browser navigation

Elements of HTML forms

HTML forms are composed with different types of elements, including `<form>`, `<input>`, `<button>`, and `<label>` as shown in the following diagram. Web developers use these elements to design the web page to display data or accept data from users. The developers write HTML code for web pages defining these elements. However, as an end user, we see these elements as the **Graphical User Interface (GUI)** controls such as textboxes, labels, buttons, checkboxes, and radio buttons. The HTML code is hidden from the end users.

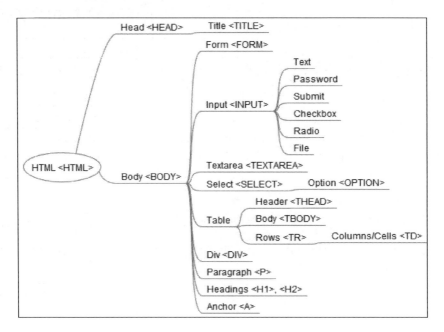

Selenium WebDriver provides broad support for automating interaction with these elements as well as checking the functionality of the application.

Understanding the WebDriver class

The `WebDriver` class provides a number of properties or attributes for browser interaction. We can use the properties and methods of the `WebDriver` class to interact with the browser window, alerts, frames and pop-up windows. It also provides features to automate browser navigation, access cookies, capture screenshots, and so on. In this chapter, we will explore some of the most important features of the `WebDriver` class. The following table covers some of the most important properties and methods that we will be using in the rest of the book.

For a complete list of properties and methods visit
`http://selenium.googlecode.com/git/`
`docs/api/py/webdriver_remote/selenium.`
`webdriver.remote.webdriver.html#module-`
`selenium.webdriver.remote.webdriver.`

Properties of the WebDriver class

The `WebDriver` class implements the following properties for accessing the browser:

Property/attribute	Description	Example
`current_url`	This gets the URL of the current page displayed in the browser	`driver.current_url`
`current_window_handle`	This gets the handle of the current window	`driver.current_window_handle`
`name`	This gets the name of the underlying browser for this instance	`driver.name`
`orientation`	This gets the current orientation of the device	`driver.orientation`
`page_source`	This gets the source of the current page	`driver.page_source`
`title`	This gets the title of the current page	`driver.title`
`window_handles`	This gets the handles of all windows within the current session	`driver.window_handles`

Methods of the WebDriver class

The `WebDriver` class implements various methods to interact with the browser window, web pages, and the elements on these pages. Here is a list of some important methods:

Method	Description	Argument	Example
`back()`	This goes one step backward in the browser history in the current session.		`driver.back()`
`close()`	This closes the current browser window.		`driver.close()`

Method	Description	Argument	Example
`forward()`	This goes one step forward in the browser history in the current session.		`driver.forward()`
`get(url)`	This navigates and loads a web page in the current browser session.	`url` is the address of the website or web page to navigate	`driver.get("http://www.google.com")`
`maximize_window()`	This maximizes the current browser window.		`driver.maximize_window()`
`quit()`	This quits the driver and closes all the associated windows.		`driver.quit()`
`refresh()`	This refreshes the current page displayed in the browser.		`driver.refresh()`
`switch_to.active_element()`	This returns the element with focus or the *body* if nothing else has focus.		`driver.switch_to_active_element()`
`Switch.to_alert()`	This switches the focus to an alert on the page.		`driver.switch_to_alert()`
`switch_to.default_content()`	This switches the focus to the default frame.		`driver.switch_to_default_content()`
`switch_to.frame(frame_reference)`	This switches the focus to the specified frame, by index, name, or web element. This method also works on IFRAMES.	`frame_reference`: This is the name of the window to switch to, an integer representing the index, or a web element that is a frame to switch to	`driver.switch_to_frame('frame_name')`

Method	Description	Argument	Example
`switch_to.window(window_name)`	This switches focus to the specified window.	`window_name` is the name or window handle of the window to switch to.	`driver.switch_to_window('main')`
`implicitly_wait(time_to_wait)`	This sets a sticky timeout to implicitly wait for an element to be found, or a command to complete. This method only needs to be called one time per session. To set the timeout for calls to `execute_async_script`, see `set_script_timeout`.	`time_to_wait` is the amount of time to wait (in seconds).	
`set_page_load_timeout(time_to_wait)`	This sets the amount of time to wait for a page load to complete.	`time_to_wait` is the amount of time to wait (in seconds).	`driver.set_page_load_timeout(30)`
`set_script_timeout(time_to_wait)`	This sets the amount of time that the script should wait during an `execute_async_script` call before throwing an error.	`time_to_wait` is the amount of time to wait (in seconds).	`driver.set_script_timeout(30)`

Understanding the WebElement class

We can interact with elements on a web page using the `WebElement` class. We can interact with a textbox, text area, button, radio buttons, checkbox, table, table row, table cell, div, and so on using the `WebElement` class.

The `WebElemet` class provides a number of properties or attributes and methods to interact with the elements. The next table covers some of the most important properties and methods that we will be using in the rest of the book. For a complete list of properties and methods, visit `http://selenium.googlecode.com/git/docs/api/py/webdriver_remote/selenium.webdriver.remote.webelement.html#module-selenium.webdriver.remote.webelement`.

Properties of the WebElement class

The WebElement class implements the following properties:

Property/attribute	Description	Example
size	This gets the size of the element	element.size
tag_name	This gets this element's HTML tag name	element.tag_name
text	This gets the text of the element	element.text

Methods of the WebElement class

The WebElement class implements the following methods:

Method	Description	Argument	Example
clear()	This clears the content of the textbox or text area element.		element.clear()
click()	This clicks the element.		element.click()
get_attribute(name)	This gets the attribute value from the element.	name is the name of the attribute.	element.get_attribute("value") Or element.get_attribute("maxlength")
is_displayed()	This checks whether the element is visible to the user.		element.is_displayed()
is_enabled()	This checks whether the element is enabled.		element.is_enabled()
is_selected()	This checks whether the element is selected. This method is used to check the selection of a radio button or checkbox.		element.is_selected()
send_keys(*value)	This simulates typing into the element.	Value is a string for typing or setting form fields.	element.send_keys("foo")

Method	Description	Argument	Example
submit()	This submits a form. If you call this method on an element, it will submit the parent form.		element.submit()
value_of_css_ property (property_name)	This gets the value of a CSS property.	property_ name is the name of the CSS property.	element.value_of_ css_property ("background- color")

Working with forms, textboxes, checkboxes, and radio buttons

We can use the WebElement class to automate the interaction on various HTML controls such as entering text in a textbox, clicking on a button, selecting an option in a checkbox or radio button, getting text and attribute values from the element, and more.

We saw the properties and methods provided by the WebElement class earlier in the chapter. In this section, we will use the WebElement class and its properties and methods to automate the create account feature of the sample application. So, let's create a test that validates the creation of a new user account in the sample application. We will fill out the form as shown in the following screenshot and submit our request. The system should then create a new user account:

As you can see from the preceding screenshot, we need to fill out five textboxes and select a checkbox for the newsletter.

1. First, create a new test class `RegisterNewUser` as shown in the following code:

```
from selenium import webdriver
import unittest

class RegisterNewUser(unittest.TestCase):
    def setUp(self):
        self.driver = webdriver.Firefox
        self.driver.implicitly_wait(30)
        self.driver.maximize_window()

        # navigate to the application home page
        self.driver.get("http://demo.magentocommerce.com/")
```

2. Add a test, `test_register_new_user(self)`, to the `RegisterNewUser` class.

3. To open the login page, we need to click on the **Log In** link on the home page. The code for the **Log In** button is as follows:

```
    def test_register_new_user(self):
        driver = self.driver

        # click on Log In link to open Login page
        driver.find_element_by_link_text("Log In").click()
```

Checking whether the element is displayed and enabled

The `is_displayed()` method returns TRUE if the element is visible on the screen (the visible attribute is set to TRUE), otherwise it will return FALSE. Similarly, the `is_enabled()` method returns TRUE if the element is enabled, that is, the user can perform actions such as click, enter text, and so on. This method returns FALSE if element is disabled.

The customer login page has options to log into the system as registered users or create an account for new users. We can check whether the **Create an Account** button is displayed to the user and it is enabled using the `is_displayed()` and `is_enabled()` methods of the `WebElement` class. Add the steps given in the following code to the test:

```
# get the Create Account button
        create_account_button = driver.find_element_by_xpath("//
button[@title='Create an Account']")
```

```
# check Create Account button is displayed and enabled
self.assertTrue(create_account_button.is_displayed() and
                create_account_button.is_enabled())
```

We want to test the `Create an Account` functionality, so let's click on the **Create an Account** button. This will display the **Create New Customer Account** page. We can use the `WebDriver` class's `title` property to check whether the page title matches with what we expected, as shown in the following code:

```
# click on Create Account button. This will display
# new account
create_account_button.click()

# check title
self.assertEquals("Create New Customer Account -
  Magento Commerce Demo Store", driver.title)
```

On the **Create New Customer Account** page, locate all the elements using the `find_element_by_*` methods as follows:

```
# get all the fields from Create an Account form
first_name = driver.find_element_by_id("firstname")
last_name = driver.find_element_by_id("lastname")
email_address = driver.find_element_by_id("email_address")
news_letter_subscription =
  driver.find_element_by_id("is_subscribed")
password = driver.find_element_by_id("password")
confirm_password = driver.find_element_by_id("confirmation")
submit_button =
  driver.find_element_by_xpath("//button[@title='Submit']")
```

Finding the element attribute value

The `get_attribute()` method can be used to get the attribute values defined for an element. For example, there is a test that says the firstname and lastname textbox should have their max length defined to 255 characters. Here is the HTML code for the `firstname` textbox, where a `maxlength` attribute is defined and its value is `255` as shown in the following code:

```
<input type="text" id="firstname" name="firstname" value=""
  title="First Name" maxlength="255" class="input-text
  required-entry">
```

We can assert the `maxlength` attribute using the `get_attribute()` method of `WebElement` with the following steps:

1. We need to pass the name of the attribute as an argument to the `get_attribute()` method:

   ```
   # check maxlength of first name and last name textbox
   self.assertEqual("255", first_name.get_
   attribute("maxlength"))
   self.assertEqual("255", last_name.get_
   attribute("maxlength"))
   ```

2. Add the following steps to the test to make sure all the fields are displayed and enabled for the user:

   ```
   # check all fields are enabled
   self.assertTrue(first_name.is_enabled() and last_name.
   is_enabled()
   and email_address.is_enabled() and news_letter_
   subscription.is_enabled()
   and password.is_enabled() and confirm_password.is_
   enabled()
   and submit_button.is_enabled())
   ```

Using the is_selected() method

The `is_selected()` method works with checkboxes and radio buttons. We can use this method to know whether a checkbox or radio button is selected or not.

A checkbox or radio button is selected by performing a click operation using the `click()` method of the `WebElement` class. In this example, check whether the **Sign Up for Newsletter** checkbox is unselected by default, as shown in the following code:

```
# check Sign Up for Newsletter is unchecked
self.assertFalse(news_letter_subscription.is_selected())
```

Using the clear() and send_keys() methods

The `clear()` and `send_keys()` methods of the `WebElement` class applicable to the textbox or textarea are useful to clear the contents of the element and send text values as if a real user were typing on the keyboard. The `send_keys()` method takes the text to be entered in the element as an argument. Let's consider the following steps:

1. Let's add the given code to fill the fields using the `send_keys()` method:

   ```
   # fill out all the fields
   first_name.send_keys("Test")
   last_name.send_keys("User1")
   ```

```
        news_letter_subscription.click()
        email_address.send_keys("TestUser_150214_2200@example.
com")

        password.send_keys("tester")
        confirm_password.send_keys("tester")
```

2. Finally, check whether the user is created by checking the welcome message. We can get the text from an element using the `text` property of the `WebElement` class:

```
        # check new user is registered
        self.assertEqual("Hello, Test User1!", driver.find_
element_by_css_selector("p.hello > strong").text)
        self.assertTrue(driver.find_element_by_link_text("Log
Out").is_displayed())
```

3. Here is a complete test for the `Create An Account` functionality. Run this test and you will see all the operations on the **Create An Account** page:

```
from selenium import webdriver
from time import gmtime, strftime
import unittest


class RegisterNewUser(unittest.TestCase):
    def setUp(self):
        self.driver = webdriver.Firefox()
        self.driver.implicitly_wait(30)
        self.driver.maximize_window()

        # navigate to the application home page
        self.driver.get("http://demo.magentocommerce.com/")

    def test_register_new_user(self):
        driver = self.driver

        # click on Log In link to open Login page
        driver.find_element_by_link_text("ACCOUNT").click()
        driver.find_element_by_link_text("My
          Account").click()

        # get the Create Account button
        create_account_button = \
            driver.find_element_by_link_text("CREATE AN
                ACCOUNT")

        # check Create Account button is displayed
        # and enabled
```

```python
self.assertTrue(create_account_button.
  is_displayed() and
  create_account_button.is_enabled())

# click on Create Account button. This will
# display new account
create_account_button.click()

# check title
self.assertEquals("Create New Customer Account",
  driver.title)

# get all the fields from Create an Account form
first_name = driver.find_element_by_id("firstname")
last_name = driver.find_element_by_id("lastname")
email_address =
  driver.find_element_by_id("email_address")
password = driver.find_element_by_id("password")
confirm_password =
  driver.find_element_by_id("confirmation")
news_letter_subscription =
  driver.find_element_by_id("is_subscribed")
submit_button = driver.\
    find_element_by_xpath
      ("//button[@title='Register']")

# check maxlength of first name and
# last name textbox
self.assertEqual("255", first_name.get_
  attribute("maxlength"))
self.assertEqual("255", last_name.get_
  attribute("maxlength"))

# check all fields are enabled
self.assertTrue(first_name.is_enabled()
  and last_name.is_enabled()
  and email_address.is_enabled() and
  news_letter_subscription.is_enabled() and
  password.is_enabled() and
  confirm_password.is_enabled()
  and submit_button.is_enabled())

# check Sign Up for Newsletter is unchecked
self.assertFalse(news_letter_subscription.
  is_selected())

user_name = "user_" + strftime
  ("%Y%m%d%H%M%S", gmtime())
```

```
        # fill out all the fields
        first_name.send_keys("Test")
        last_name.send_keys(user_name)
        news_letter_subscription.click()
        email_address.send_keys(user_name + "@example.com")
        password.send_keys("tester")
        confirm_password.send_keys("tester")

        # click Submit button to submit the form
        submit_button.click()

        # check new user is registered
        self.assertEqual("Hello, Test " + user_name + "!",
          driver.find_element_by_css_selector("p.hello >
          strong").text)
        driver.find_element_by_link_text("ACCOUNT").click()
        self.assertTrue(driver.find_element_by_link_text
          ("Log Out").is_displayed())

    def tearDown(self):
        self.driver.quit()

if __name__ == "__main__":
    unittest.main(verbosity=2)
```

Working with dropdowns and lists

Selenium WebDriver provides a special `Select` class to interact with the lists and dropdowns on a web page. For example, in the demo application, you can see a dropdown to select the language for the store. You can choose and set a language for the store as shown in the following screenshot:

Dropdowns or lists are implemented with the `<select>` element in HTML. The options or choices are implemented with the `<options>` element within a `<select>` element as shown in the following HTML code:

```
<select id="select-language" title="Your Language"
    onchange="window.location.href=this.value">
    <option value="http://demo.magentocommerce.com/?
        ___store=default&amp;___from_store=default"
      selected="selected">English</option>
    <option value="http://demo.magentocommerce.com/?
        ___store=french&amp;___from_store=default">French</option>
    <option value="http://demo.magentocommerce.com/?
        ___store=german&amp;___from_store=default">German</option>
</select>
```

Each `<option>` element has its attribute value defined and text that the user will see. For example, in the following code, the `<option>` value is set to the URL of the store and the text is set to the language, that is, `French`:

```
<option value="http://demo.magentocommerce.com/customer/
    account/create/?___store=french&amp;
    ___from_store=default">French</option>
```

Understanding the Select class

The `Select` class is a special class in Selenium that is used to interact with dropdowns or lists. It offers various methods and properties for user interaction.

The following table lists all the properties and methods from the `Select` class. You can find similar information at `http://selenium.googlecode.com/git/docs/api/py/webdriver_support/selenium.webdriver.support.select.html#module-selenium.webdriver.support.select`.

Properties of the Select class

The Select class implements the following properties:

Property/attribute	Description	Example
all_selected_options	This gets a list of all the selected options belonging to the dropdown or list	select_element.all_selected_options
first_selected_option	This gets the first selected / currently selected option from the dropdown or list	select_element.first_selected_option
options	This gets a list of all options from the dropdown or list	select_element.options

Methods of the Select class

The Select class implements the following methods:

Method	Description	Argument	Example
deselect_all()	This clears all the selected entries from a multiselect dropdown or list		select_element.deselect_all()
deselect_by_index(index)	This deselects the option at the given index from the dropdown or list	index is the index of the option to be deselected	select_element.deselect_by_index(1)
deselect_by_value(value)	This deselects all options that have a value matching the argument from the dropdown or list	value is the value attribute of the option to be deselected	select_element.deselect_by_value("foo")
deselect_by_visible_text(text)	This deselects all the options that display text matching the argument from the dropdown or list	text is the text value of the option to be deselected	select_element.deselect_by_visible_text("bar")
select_by_index(index)	This selects an option at the given index from the dropdown or list	index is the index of the option to be selected	select_element.select_by_index(1)

Method	Description	Argument	Example
`select_by_value(value)`	This selects all the options that have a value matching the argument from the dropdown or list	`value` is the value attribute of the option to be selected	`select_element.select_by_value("foo")`
`select_by_visible_text(text)`	This selects all the options that display the text matching the argument from the dropdown or list	`text` is the text value of the option to be selected	`select_element.select_by_visible_text("bar")`

Let's explore these properties and methods to test the language features of the demo application. We will add a new test to the home page test that we built in the previous chapters. This test checks whether the user has eight languages to select from. We will use the `options` property to first check the number of options and then get the text of each option in a list and check that list with an expected option list, as shown in the following code:

```python
def test_language_options(self):
    # list of expected values in Language dropdown
    exp_options = ["ENGLISH", "FRENCH", "GERMAN"]

    # empty list for capturing actual options displayed
    # in the dropdown
    act_options = []

    # get the Your language dropdown as instance of Select class
    select_language = \
        Select(self.driver.find_element_by_id("select-language"))

    # check number of options in dropdown
    self.assertEqual(2, len(select_language.options))

    # get options in a list
    for option in select_language.options:
        act_options.append(option.text)

    # check expected options list with actual options list
    self.assertListEqual(exp_options, act_options)

    # check default selected option is English
```

```
self.assertEqual("ENGLISH", select_language.first_selected_option.
text)

# select an option using select_by_visible text
select_language.select_by_visible_text("German")

# check store is now German
self.assertTrue("store=german" in self.driver.current_url)

# changing language will refresh the page,
# we need to get find language dropdown once again
select_language = \
    Select(self.driver.find_element_by_id("select-language"))
    select_language.select_by_index(0)
```

The `options` property returns all the `<option>` elements defined for a dropdown or list. Each item in the options list is an instance of the `WebElement` class.

We can also check the default/current selected option using the `first_selected_option` property.

 The `all_selected_options` property is used to test multiselect dropdowns or lists.

Finally, select an item and check whether the store URL is changed based on the language selection using the following code:

```
# select an option using select_by_visible text
select_language.select_by_visible_text("German")

# check store is now German
self.assertTrue("store=german" in self.driver.current_url)
```

Option(s) can be selected by their index (that is, their position in the list), by the value attribute or by the visible text. The `Select` class offers various `select_` methods to select the options. In this example, we used the `select_by_visible_text()` method to select an option. We can also deselect options using various `deselect_` methods.

Working with alerts and pop-up windows

Developers use JavaScript alerts or model dialogs to inform users about validation errors, warnings, to give a response for an action, accept an input value, and more. In this section, we will see how to handle alerts and pop-up windows with Selenium.

Understanding the Alert class

Selenium WebDriver provides the `Alert` class to handle JavaScript alerts. The `Alert` class contains methods for accepting, dismissing, inputting, and getting text from alerts.

Properties of the Alert class

The `Alert` class implements the following property:

Property/attribute	Description	Example
text	This gets text from the alert window	alert.text

Methods of the Alert class

The `Alert` class implements the following methods:

Method	Description	Argument	Example
accept()	This will accept the JavaScript alert box that is click on the **OK** button		alert.accept()
dismiss()	This will dismiss the JavaScript alert box that is click on the **Cancel** button		alert.dismiss()
send_keys(*value)	This simulates typing into the element	value is a string for typing or setting form fields	alert.send_keys("foo")

In the demo application, you can find the use of alerts to inform or warn the user. For example, when you add products for comparison and then remove one of the products or all the products from the comparison, the application shows you an alert similar to the one shown in following screenshot:

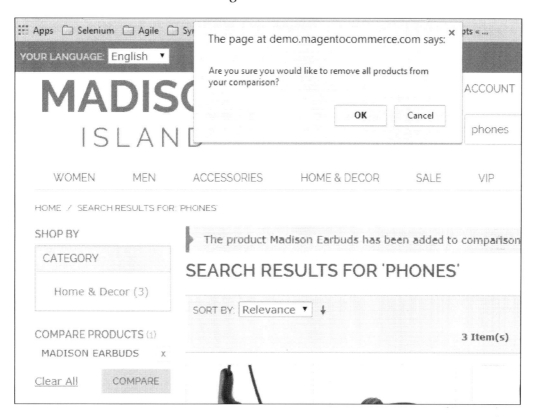

We will implement a test that checks whether the **Clear All** option in the **COMPARE PRODUCTS** feature displays an alert window to the users asking whether they are sure about the removal of products from the comparison.

Create a new test class, `CompareProducts`, and add steps to search and add a product to compare as shown in the following code snippet:

```
from selenium import webdriver
import unittest


class CompareProducts(unittest.TestCase):
    def setUp(self):
        self.driver = webdriver.Firefox()
```

```
        self.driver.implicitly_wait(30)
        self.driver.maximize_window()
        self.driver.get("http://demo.magentocommerce.com/")

    def test_compare_products_removal_alert(self):
        # get the search textbox
        search_field = self.driver.find_element_by_name("q")
        search_field.clear()

        # enter search keyword and submit
        search_field.send_keys("phones")
        search_field.submit()

        # click the Add to compare link
        self.driver.\
            find_element_by_link_text("Add to Compare").click()
```

Once a product is added for comparison by clicking on the **Add to Compare** link, you will see the product added to the **COMPARE PRODUCTS** section. You can also add another product for comparison. If you want to remove all products from comparison, you can do so by clicking on the **Clear All** link from the **COMPARE PRODUCTS** section. You will get an alert asking you whether you want to clear all the products. We can handle this alert using the `Alert` class. The `switch_to_alert()` method of the `WebDriver` class returns the instance of `Alert`. We can use this instance to read the message displayed on the alert and accept that alert, by clicking on the **OK** button or dismissing the alert, by clicking on the **Cancel** button. Add the following code to the test. This part reads and checks the alert message and then accepts the alert by calling the `accept()` method:

```
        # click on Remove this item link, this will display
        # an alert to the user
        self.driver.find_element_by_link_text("Clear All").click()

        # switch to the alert
        alert = self.driver.switch_to_alert()

        # get the text from alert
        alert_text = alert.text

        # check alert text
        self.assertEqual("Are you sure you would like to
          remove all products from your comparison?", alert_text)

        # click on Ok button
        alert.accept()
```

```
    def tearDown(self):
        self.driver.quit()

if __name__ == "__main__":
    unittest.main()
```

Automating browser navigation

Browsers provide various navigation methods to access the web pages from the browser history or by refreshing the current page and so on with the back, forward, refresh/reload buttons on the browser window's toolbar. The Selenium WebDriver API provides access to these buttons with various navigation methods. We can test the behavior of the application when these methods are used. The `WebDriver` class provides the following methods to perform browser navigation such as back, forward, and refresh:

Method	Description	Argument	Example
back()	This goes one step backward in the browser history of the current session	None	driver.back()
forward()	This goes one step forward in the browser history of the current session	None	driver.forward()
refresh()	This refreshes the current page displayed in the browser	None	driver.refresh()

Here is an example that uses the browser navigation API to navigate the history and validate the state of the application:

```
import unittest
from selenium import webdriver
from selenium.webdriver.support.ui import WebDriverWait
from selenium.webdriver.support import expected_conditions

class NavigationTest(unittest.TestCase):
    def setUp(self):
        # create a new Firefox session
        self.driver = webdriver.Chrome()
        self.driver.implicitly_wait(30)
        self.driver.maximize_window()
```

```python
    # navigate to the application home page
    self.driver.get("http://www.google.com")

def testBrowserNavigation(self):
    driver = self.driver
    # get the search textbox
    search_field = driver.find_element_by_name("q")
    search_field.clear()

    # enter search keyword and submit
    search_field.send_keys("selenium webdriver")
    search_field.submit()

    se_wd_link = driver.find_element_by_link_text
        ("Selenium WebDriver")
    se_wd_link.click()
    self.assertEqual("Selenium WebDriver", driver.title)

    driver.back()
    self.assertTrue(WebDriverWait(self.driver, 10)
        .until(expected_conditions.title_is
            ("selenium webdriver - Google Search")))

    driver.forward()
    self.assertTrue(WebDriverWait(self.driver, 10)
        .until(expected_conditions.title_is
            ("Selenium WebDriver")))

    driver.refresh()
    self.assertTrue(WebDriverWait(self.driver, 10)
        .until(expected_conditions.title_is
            ("Selenium WebDriver")))

def tearDown(self):
    # close the browser window
    self.driver.quit()

if __name__ == '__main__':
    unittest.main()
```

Summary

In this chapter, you were introduced to the Selenium WebDriver API for interacting with various elements on a page. The Selenium WebDriver API offers various classes, properties, and methods to simulate the user actions and check the application states. We looked at various methods to automate elements such as textboxes, buttons, checkboxes, and dropdowns.

We created some tests that deal with alerts. We also looked at using browser navigation method and tested the navigation between pages.

In the next chapter, we will explore the Selenium API to handle synchronizing tests. This will help us in building reliable tests with Selenium.

5
Synchronizing Tests

Building robust and reliable tests is one of the critical success factors of automated UI testing. However, you will come across situations where testing conditions differ from one test to another. When your script searches for elements or a certain state of application and it cannot find these elements anymore because the application starts responding slowly due to sudden resource constraints or network latency, the tests report false negative results. We need to match the speed of the test script with the application's speed by introducing delays in the test script. In other words, we need to sync the script with the application's response. WebDriver offers implicit and explicit waits to synchronize tests.

In this chapter, you will learn about the following topics:

- Using implicit and explicit wait
- When to use implicit and explicit wait
- Using expected conditions
- Creating a custom wait condition

Using implicit wait

The implicit wait offers a generic way to synchronize the entire test or group of steps in WebDriver. Implicit wait is useful in dealing with situations where the application's response time is inconsistent due to network speed or applications that use dynamically rendered elements with Ajax calls.

When we set an implicit wait on WebDriver, it polls or searches the DOM for a certain amount of time to find an element or elements if they are not immediately available. By default, the implicit wait timeout is set to `0`.

Once set, the implicit wait is set for the life of the WebDriver instance or for the entire duration of the test, and the WebDriver applies this implicit wait for all the steps that find the elements on the page unless we set it back to 0.

The `webdriver` class provides the `implicitly_wait()` method to configure timeout. We created a `SearchProductTest` test in *Chapter 2, Writing Tests Using unittest*. We will modify this test and add an implicit wait with timeout of 10 seconds in the `setUp()` method as shown in following code example. When the test is executed, WebDriver will wait for up to 10 seconds if it doesn't find an element. When it reaches the timeout, that is, 10 seconds in this example, it will throw a `NoSuchElementException`.

```python
import unittest
from selenium import webdriver


class SearchProductTest(unittest.TestCase):
    def setUp(self):
        # create a new Firefox session
        self.driver = webdriver.Firefox()
        self.driver.implicitly_wait(30)
        self.driver.maximize_window()

        # navigate to the application home page
        self.driver.get("http://demo.magentocommerce.com/")

    def test_search_by_category(self):

        # get the search textbox
        self.search_field = self.driver.find_element_by_name("q")
        self.search_field.clear()

        # enter search keyword and submit
        self.search_field.send_keys("phones")
        self.search_field.submit()

        # get all the anchor elements which have product names
        # displayed currently on result page using
        # find_elements_by_xpath method
        products = self.driver\
            .find_elements_by_xpath
                ("//h2[@class='product-name']/a")

        # check count of products shown in results
        self.assertEqual(2, len(products))
```

```
    def tearDown(self):
        # close the browser window
        self.driver.quit()

if __name__ == '__main__':
    unittest.main(verbosity=2)
```

 It is better to avoid using an implicit wait in tests and try to handle synchronization issues with an explicit wait, which provides more control when compared to an implicit wait.

Using explicit wait

The explicit wait is another wait mechanism available in WebDriver to synchronize tests. Explicit wait provides a better control when compared to implicit wait. Unlike an implicit wait, we can use a set of predefined or custom conditions for the script to wait for before proceeding with further steps.

An explicit wait can only be implemented in specific cases where script synchronization is needed. WebDriver provides the `WebDriverWait` and `expected_conditions` classes to implement an explicit wait.

The `expected_conditions` class provides a set of predefined conditions to wait for before proceeding further in the code.

Let's create a simple test that uses explicit wait with an expected condition for visibility of an element, as shown in the following code:

```
from selenium import webdriver
from selenium.webdriver.common.by import By
from selenium.webdriver.support.ui import WebDriverWait
from selenium.webdriver.support import expected_conditions
import unittest


class ExplicitWaitTests(unittest.TestCase):
    def setUp(self):
        self.driver = webdriver.Firefox()
        self.driver.get("http://demo.magentocommerce.com/")

    def test_account_link(self):
        WebDriverWait(self.driver, 10)\
            .until(lambda s: s.find_element_by_id("select-
                language").get_attribute("length") == "3")
```

```
    account = WebDriverWait(self.driver, 10)\
        .until(expected_conditions.
         visibility_of_element_located
         ((By.LINK_TEXT, "ACCOUNT")))
    account.click()

def tearDown(self):
    self.driver.quit()

if __name__ == "__main__":
    unittest.main(verbosity=2)
```

In this test, explicit wait is used to wait until the **Log In** link is visible in the DOM, using the expected `visibility_of_element_located` condition. This condition requires the locator strategy and locator details for the element we want to wait for. The script will wait for a maximum of 10 seconds looking for the element to be visible. Once the element is visible with the specified locator, the expected condition will return the located element back to the script.

If an element is not visible with the specified locator in the given timeout, a `TimeoutException` will be raised.

The expected condition class

The following table shows some common conditions along with examples that we frequently come across when automating web browsers supported by the `expected_conditions` class:

Expected condition	Description	Argument	Example
`element_to_be_clickable (locator)`	This will wait for an element to be located and be visible and enabled so that it can be clicked. This method returns the element that is located back to the test.	`locator:` This is a tuple of `(by, locator)`.	`WebDriverWait(self. driver, 10). until(expected_ conditions.element_ to_be_clickable((By. NAME,"is_subscribed")))`

Expected condition	Description	Argument	Example

`element_to_be_selected(element)`	This will wait until a specified element is selected.	`element:` This is the WebElement.	`subscription = self.driver.find_element_by_name("is_subscribed")`
			
			`WebDriverWait(self.driver, 10).until(expected_conditions.element_to_be_selected(subscription))`

`invisibility_of_element_located(locator)`	This will wait for an element that is either invisible or is not present on the DOM.	`locator:` This is a tuple of `(by, locator)`.	`WebDriverWait(self.driver, 10).until(expected_conditions.invisibility_of_element_located((By.ID,"loading_banner")))`
`presence_of_all_elements_located(locator)`	This will wait until at least one element for the matching locator is present on the web page. This method returns the list of WebElements once they are located.	`locator:` This is a tuple of `(by, locator)`.	`WebDriverWait(self.driver, 10).until(expected_conditions.presence_of_all_elements_located((By.CLASS_NAME,"input-text")))`
`presence_of_element_located(locator)`	This will wait until an element for the matching locator is present on a web page or available on the DOM. This method returns an element once it is located.	`locator:` This is a tuple of `(by, locator)`.	`WebDriverWait(self.driver, 10).until(expected_conditions.presence_of_element_located((By.ID,"search")))`
`text_to_be_present_in_element(locator, text_)`	This will wait until an element is located and has the given text.	`locator:` This is a tuple of `(by, locator)`. `text:` This is the text to be checked.	`WebDriverWait(self.driver,10).until(expected_conditions.text_to_be_present_in_element((By.ID,"select-language"),"English"))`

Expected condition	Description	Argument	Example
`title_contains(title)`	This will wait for the page tile to contain a case-sensitive substring. This method returns `true` if the tile matches, `false` otherwise.	`title`: This is the substring of the title to check.	`WebDriverWait(self.driver, 10).until(expected_conditions.title_contains("Create New Customer Account"))`
`title_is(title)`	This will wait for the page tile to be equal to the expected title. This method returns `true` if the tile matches, `false` otherwise.	`title`: This is the title of the page.	`WebDriverWait(self.driver, 10).until(expected_conditions.title_is("Create New Customer Account - Magento Commerce Demo Store"))`

`visibility_of(element)`	This will wait until an element is present in DOM, is visible, and its width and height are greater than zero.
	
	This method returns the (same) WebElement once it becomes visible.
		`element`: This is the WebElement.	`first_name = self.driver.find_element_by_id("firstname")`
			
			`WebDriverWait(self.driver, 10).until(expected_conditions.visibility_of(first_name))`

`visibility_of_element_located(locator)`	This will wait until an element to be located is present in DOM, is visible, and its width and height are greater than zero. This method returns the WebElement once it becomes visible.	`locator`: This is a tuple of (by, locator).	`WebDriverWait(self.driver, 10).until(expected_conditions.visibility_of_element_located((By.ID, "firstname")))`

You can find a complete list of expected conditions at `http://selenium.googlecode.com/git/docs/api/py/webdriver_support/selenium.webdriver.support.expected_conditions.html#module-selenium.webdriver.support.expected_conditions`.

Let's explore few more examples of expected conditions in the upcoming sections.

Waiting for an element to be enabled

As we have seen earlier, the `expected_conditons` class provides a variety of wait conditions that we can implement in our scripts. In the following example, we will wait for an element to be enabled or made clickable. We can use this condition in Ajax-heavy applications where form fields are enabled or disabled based on other form field values or filters. In this example, we click on the **Log In** link and then wait for the **Create an Account** button to become clickable, which is displayed on the login page. We will then click on the **Create an Account** button and wait for the next page to be displayed.

```
def test_create_new_customer(self):
    # click on Log In link to open Login page
    self.driver.find_element_by_link_text("ACCOUNT").click()

    # wait for My Account link in Menu
    my_account = WebDriverWait(self.driver, 10)\
        .until(expected_conditions.visibility_of_element_located((By.
    LINK_TEXT, "My Account")))
    my_account.click()

    # get the Create Account button
    create_account_button = WebDriverWait(self.driver, 10)\
        .until(expected_conditions.element_to_be_clickable((By.LINK_
        TEXT, "CREATE AN ACCOUNT")))

    # click on Create Account button. This will displayed new account
    create_account_button.click()
    WebDriverWait(self.driver, 10)\
        .until(expected_conditions.title_contains("Create New Customer
        Account"))
```

We can wait and check for an element to be enabled by using the `element_to_be_clickable` condition. This requires the locator strategy and locator value. It returns the located element back to the script when that element becomes clickable or, in other words, enabled.

The preceding tests also wait for the creating new customer account page to be loaded by checking the title with the specified text. We used the `title_contains` condition that checks to make sure that the substring matches with the title of the page.

Waiting for alerts

We can also use explicit wait on alerts and frames. A complex JavaScript processing or backend request might take time to display the alert to the user. This can be handled by the expected `alert_is_present` condition in the following way:

```python
from selenium import webdriver
from selenium.webdriver.support.ui import WebDriverWait
from selenium.webdriver.common.by import By
from selenium.webdriver.support import expected_conditions
import unittest


class CompareProducts(unittest.TestCase):
    def setUp(self):
        self.driver = webdriver.Firefox()
        self.driver.get("http://demo.magentocommerce.com/")

    def test_compare_products_removal_alert(self):
        # get the search textbox
        search_field = self.driver.find_element_by_name("q")
        search_field.clear()

        # enter search keyword and submit
        search_field.send_keys("phones")
        search_field.submit()

        # click the Add to compare link
        self.driver.\
            find_element_by_link_text("Add to Compare").click()

        # wait for Clear All link to be visible
        clear_all_link = WebDriverWait(self.driver, 10)\
            .until(expected_conditions.visibility_of_element_
            located((By.LINK_TEXT, "Clear All")))

        # click on Clear All link,
        # this will display an alert to the user
        clear_all_link.click()

        # wait for the alert to present
        alert = WebDriverWait(self.driver, 10)\
            .until(expected_conditions.alert_is_present())

        # get the text from alert
        alert_text = alert.text
```

```
        # check alert text
        self.assertEqual("Are you sure you would like
    to remove all products from your comparison?", alert_text)
        # click on Ok button
        alert.accept()

    def tearDown(self):
        self.driver.quit()

if __name__ == "__main__":
    unittest.main(verbosity=2)
```

The preceding test validates the removal of products from the product comparison feature of the application. Users are sent a confirmation alert when they remove a product from the comparison. The `alert_is_present` condition is used to check if the alert is displayed to the user and returned back to the script for the upcoming actions. The script will wait for 10 seconds checking for the presence of the alert, otherwise it will raise an exception.

Implementing custom wait conditions

As we have seen earlier, the `expected_conditions` class provides various predefined conditions to wait. We can also build custom conditions with `WebDriverWait`. This becomes useful when there is no suitable expected condition available for which to wait.

Let's modify one of the tests we created earlier in this chapter and implement a custom wait condition to check the number of the drop-down items:

```
def testLoginLink(self):
    WebDriverWait(self.driver, 10).until
        (lambda s: s.find_element_by_id
        ("select-language").get_attribute("length") == "3")

    login_link = WebDriverWait
        (self.driver, 10).until(expected_conditions.
        visibility_of_element_located((By.LINK_TEXT,"Log In")))
        login_link.click();
```

We can implement custom wait conditions with `WebDriverWait` using the Python lambda expressions. In this example, the script will wait for 10 seconds until the **Select Language** dropdown has eight options for selection. This condition is useful when the dropdowns are populated by Ajax calls and the script needs to wait until all the options are available to the user for selection.

Summary

In this chapter, we recognized the need for synchronization and its importance in building highly reliable tests. We looked at the implicit wait and how to use implicit wait as a generic wait mechanism with an example. We then looked at the explicit wait that offers a more flexible way to synchronize tests. The `expected_conditions` class offers various built-in conditions for the wait. We have implemented some of these conditions.

The `WebDriverWait` class also provides a very powerful way to implement custom wait conditions over and above `expected_conditions`. We implemented a custom wait condition on a dropdown.

In the next chapter, you will learn how to implement cross-browser testing using `RemoteWebDriver` and Selenium Server for running tests on a remote machine and parallel execution with Selenium Grid.

6
Cross-browser Testing

Selenium supports cross-browser testing on multiple browser and operating system combinations. This is a very useful feature for testing web applications on various browser and operating system combinations to certify that the app is cross-browser compatible and to make sure that users do not experience problems with their choice of browsers or operating systems. Selenium WebDriver offers an ability to run tests on remote machines or distribute them against a number of operating systems and browsers running on remote machines or the cloud. So far, you have learned how to create and run tests on a local machine with various browser drivers installed as shown in the following diagram:

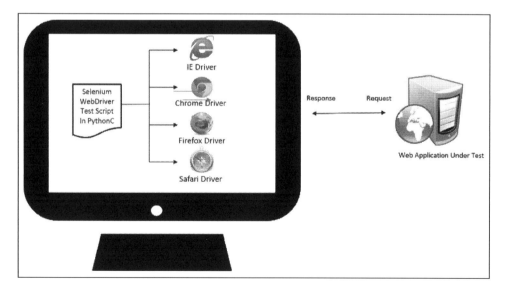

In this chapter, you will learn how to run these tests on a remote machine and then how to scale and run tests in a distributed architecture on multiple browser and operating system combinations for cross-browser testing. This saves a great amount of effort and time spent in cross-browser testing. We will cover the following aspects in this chapter:

- Downloading and using the Selenium standalone server
- How to use the `Remote` class to run tests on the Selenium standalone server
- Running tests on the Selenium standalone server
- Adding nodes to the Selenium standalone server to create a grid for distributed execution
- Running tests in the grid against multiple browser and operating system combinations
- Running tests in a cloud with Sauce Labs and BrowserStack

The Selenium standalone server

The Selenium standalone server is a component of Selenium that provides the ability to run tests on remote machines. We need to use the `RemoteWebDriver` class to connect to the Selenium standalone server to run tests on a remote machine. The `RemoteWebDriver` class listens to Selenium commands coming from test scripts using the `RemoteWebDriver` class on a designated port. Based on the configuration provided by the `RemoteWebDriver` class, the Selenium server will launch the specified browser and forward the commands to the browser. It supports almost all the browsers and mobile platforms with Appium. The following diagram shows the architecture of the Selenium server running tests on remote machines configured with different types of browsers:

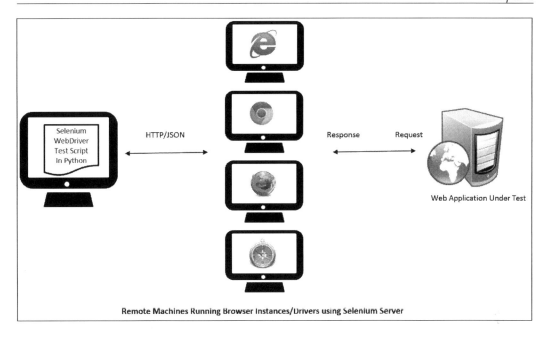

Remote Machines Running Browser Instances/Drivers using Selenium Server

Downloading the Selenium standalone server

The Selenium standalone server is available in a bundled JAR format for download at `http://docs.seleniumhq.org/download/` in the *Selenium Server (formerly the Selenium RC Server)* section. While writing this book, Selenium server Version 2.41.0 was available for download. You can simply copy the Selenium standalone server JAR file on a remote machine and start the server.

> The Selenium standalone server is a self-contained server written in Java. It requires a Java Runtime Environment (JRE) to be installed on the machine where it is run. Please make sure you have installed JRE 6 or onwards on the remote machine where you intend to run the Selenium standalone server.

Launching the Selenium standalone server

The Selenium standalone server can be launched in various modes or roles. In this section, we will launch it in a standalone mode. We can launch the server with the following command on the remote machine's command line from the directory where the server's JAR file is kept. In this example, it is launched on a Windows 8 machine by using the following command line:

```
java -jar selenium-server-standalone-2.41.0.jar
```

By default, Selenium server will start listening on port 4444 at http://<remote-machine-ip>:4444. It is possible to change the port through the command-line option while starting the server. When the server is launched, you will see the following output on the command line:

```
C:\Windows\System32\cmd.exe - java -jar selenium-server-standalone-2.41.0.jar

C:\Users\UNMESH\Downloads>java -jar selenium-server-standalone-2.41.0.jar
10 May, 2014 6:34:38 PM org.openqa.grid.selenium.GridLauncher main
INFO: Launching a standalone server
18:34:38.801 INFO - Java: Sun Microsystems Inc. 20.45-b01
18:34:38.803 INFO - OS: Windows 8 6.2 amd64
18:34:38.844 INFO - v2.41.0, with Core v2.41.0. Built from revision 3192d8a
18:34:39.125 INFO - RemoteWebDriver instances should connect to: http://127.0.0.
1:4444/wd/hub
18:34:39.128 INFO - Version Jetty/5.1.x
18:34:39.130 INFO - Started HttpContext[/selenium-server/driver,/selenium-server
/driver]
18:34:39.132 INFO - Started HttpContext[/selenium-server,/selenium-server]
18:34:39.133 INFO - Started HttpContext[/,/]
18:34:39.268 INFO - Started org.openqa.jetty.jetty.servlet.ServletHandler@2993a6
6f
18:34:39.269 INFO - Started HttpContext[/wd,/wd]
18:34:39.276 INFO - Started SocketListener on 0.0.0.0:4444
18:34:39.277 INFO - Started org.openqa.jetty.jetty.Server@5dccce3c
```

The Selenium server will be launched as an HTTP server on the remote machine and we can launch and see the server in a browser window. Launch the browser and navigate to http://<remote-machine-ip>:4444/wd/hub/static/resource/hub.html. This will display the following page in the browser window:

Now that we have the Selenium server up and running, it is time to create and run a test that we can run on the server.

Running a test on the Selenium standalone server

To run a test on Selenium server, we need to use RemoteWebDriver. The Remote class in the Selenium Python binding acts like a client and communicates with the Selenium server to run the tests on a remote machine. We need to use this class to instruct the Selenium server as to what configurations are needed to run a test on a remote machine and commands to run on selected browsers.

In addition to the Remote class, we need to set desired_capabilities, that is the browser, operating system, and any other configuration that we want to communicate to the Selenium standalone server to run the test. In this example, we will specify a platform and browser name as the desired capabilities required to run the test:

```
desired_caps = {}
desired_caps['platform'] = 'WINDOWS'
desired_caps['browserName'] = 'firefox'
```

Next, we will create an instance of the Remote class and pass desired_capabilities. When the script is executed, it will connect to the Selenium server and request the server to set up a Firefox browser running on Windows to run the test:

```
self.driver = webdriver.Remote('http://192.168.1.103:4444/wd/hub',
desired_caps)
```

Let's implement a search test that we created earlier and use the Remote class instead of the Firefox driver in the following way:

```
import unittest
from selenium import webdriver


class SearchProducts(unittest.TestCase):
    def setUp(self):

        desired_caps = {}
        desired_caps['platform'] = 'WINDOWS'
        desired_caps['browserName'] = 'firefox'

        self.driver = \
            webdriver.Remote('http://192.168.1.102:4444/wd/hub',
            desired_caps)
        self.driver.get('http://demo.magentocommerce.com/')
        self.driver.implicitly_wait(30)
        self.driver.maximize_window()
```

```
def testSearchByCategory(self):

    # get the search textbox
    self.search_field = self.driver.find_element_by_name('q')
    self.search_field.clear()

    # enter search keyword and submit
    self.search_field.send_keys('phones')
    self.search_field.submit()

    # get all the anchor elements which have product names
    # displayed currently on result page using
    # find_elements_by_xpath method
    products = self.driver\
        .find_elements_by_xpath('//h2[@class=\'product-name\']/a')

    # check count of products shown in results
    self.assertEqual(2, len(products))

def tearDown(self):
    # close the browser window
    self.driver.quit()

if __name__ == '__main__':
    unittest.main()
```

When this test is executed, you can see the console of the Selenium server. It shows the interaction between the test and the server as shown in the following screenshot. It shows which command has been executed and its status:

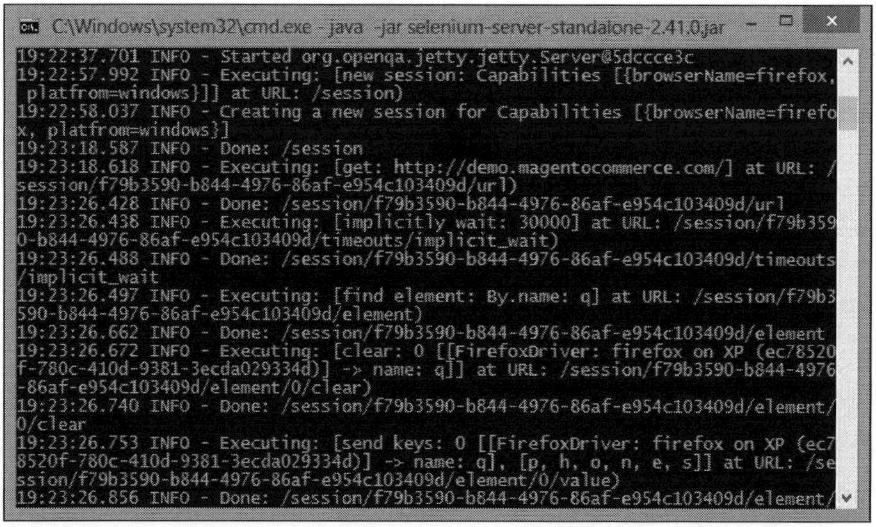

You can also navigate to `http://<remote-machine-ip>:4444/wd/hub/static/resource/hub.html`, which displays a new session being created. If you hover over the capabilities link, it displays the capabilities being used to run the tests, as shown in the following screenshot:

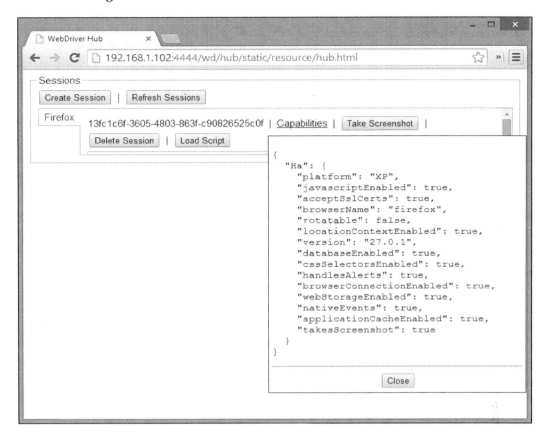

Adding support for Internet Explorer

Firefox support is bundled with the Selenium server; however, for running tests on **Internet Explorer** (IE), we need to specify the path of the IE driver executable while starting the Selenium server. This is done by specifying the executable path to the wedriver.ie.driver option in the command line as shown:

```
java -Dwebdriver.ie.driver="C:\SeDrivers\IEDriverServer.exe" -jar
selenium-server-standalone-2.41.0.jar
```

By providing the path of the IE driver, Selenium server will now launch and support IE for testing on the remote machine.

Adding support for Chrome

Similar to the IE driver executable, we need to mention the Chrome driver on the remote machine to support testing on Chrome. This is done by specifying the Chrome driver path in the webdriver.chrome.driver option as shown in following command line:

```
java -Dwebdriver.ie.driver="C:\SeDrivers\IEDriverServer.exe" -Dwebdriver.
chrome.driver="C:\SeDrivers\chromedriver.exe" -jar selenium-server-
standalone-2.41.0.jar
```

The Selenium server will now support running tests on both the Internet Explorer and Chrome on the remote machine.

Selenium Grid

Selenium Grid lets us distribute our tests across multiple physical or virtual machines in order to run tests in a distributed fashion or run them in parallel. This helps in getting a faster and more accurate feedback by cutting down the time required for running tests and speeding up cross-browser testing. We can use our existing infrastructure of virtual machines in a cloud to set up the Grid.

Selenium Grid enables us to run multiple tests in parallel, on multiple nodes or clients, in a heterogeneous environment where we can have a mixture of browser and operating system support. It makes all these nodes appear as a single instance and transparently distributes tests on the underlying infrastructure as shown in the following diagram:

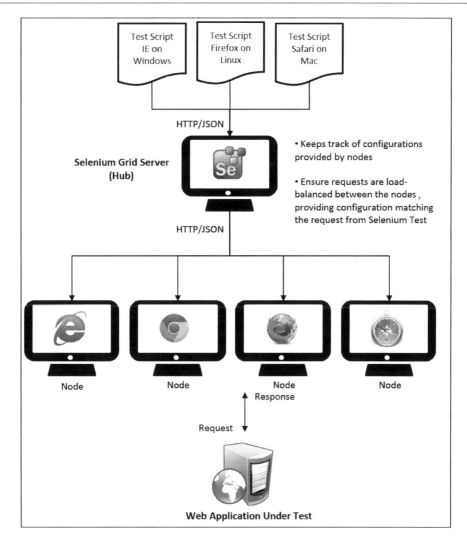

Launching Selenium server as a hub

We need to set up Selenium server as a hub to run the tests in a distributed fashion. The hub will provide all the available configurations or capabilities to tests.

The slave machines, also called as nodes, connect to the hub. Tests will use JSON wire protocol using the `Remote` class to communicate with the hub to execute the Selenium commands. You can find more about JSON wire protocol at `https://code.google.com/p/selenium/wiki/JsonWireProtocol`.

The hub acts as the central point that will receive the commands from tests and distribute them to the appropriate node or to the node matching the capabilities required by the test. Let's set up a Selenium server as a Grid and then add nodes with different browser and operating system combinations.

We can start the Selenium standalone server as a hub (also known as a Grid server) with additional arguments to the command that we used to start the server in earlier sections.

Create a new command/terminal window and navigate to the location where the Selenium server JAR is located. Start the server as a hub by typing the following command:

```
java -jar selenium-server-standalone-2.25.0.jar -port 4444 -role hub
```

We need to use the `-role` argument with the value `hub` to start the server as hub or Grid server.

In this example, the server is started on a Windows machine. It starts with the following information printed on the console:

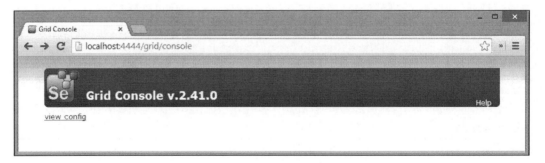

When we start the Selenium server as hub, it starts as a Grid server. We can see the Grid console in the browser as shown in the following screenshot:

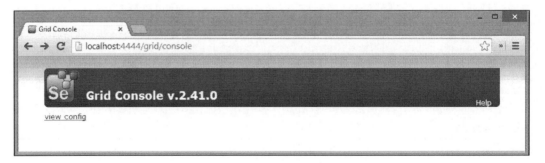

Adding nodes

Now that we have our Selenium server started as a Grid server, let's add a few node configurations to the server.

Adding an IE node

Let's begin with a node that provides Internet Explorer capabilities running on Windows. Open a new command prompt or a terminal window and navigate to the location where the Selenium server JAR is located. To launch a node and add it to the Grid, type the following command:

```
java -Dwebdriver.ie.driver="C:\SeDrivers\IEDriverServer.exe" -jar
selenium-server-standalone-2.41.0.jar -role webdriver -browser
"browserName=internet explorer,version=10,maxinstance=1,platform=WINDOWS"
-hubHost 192.168.1.103 -port 5555
```

To add the node to the Grid, we need to use the -role argument and pass webdriver as a value. We also need to pass the browser configuration for the node. This is passed through the -browser argument. In this example, we passed browserName as internet explorer, version as 10, maxinstance as 1, and platform as WINDOWS. The maxinstance value tells the Grid how many concurrent instances of the browser will be supported by the node.

To connect the node to the hub or Grid server, we need to specify the -hubHost argument with the hostname or IP address of the Grid server. Lastly, we need to specify the port on which the node will be running.

When we run the preceding command and the node is launched, the following configuration will appear on the Grid console:

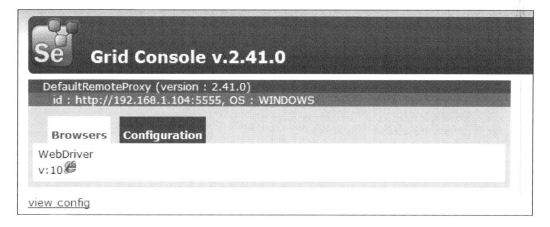

Alternatively, a node can be added by creating a configuration file in JSON format and then using the following code:

```json
{
    "class": "org.openqa.grid.common.RegistrationRequest",
    "capabilities": [
     {
     "seleniumProtocol": "WebDriver",
     "browserName": "internet explorer",
     "version": "10",
     "maxInstances": 1,
     "platform" : "WINDOWS"
     }
    ],
    "configuration": {
     "port": 5555,
     "register": true,
     "host": "192.168.1.103",
     "proxy": "org.openqa.grid.selenium.proxy.
     DefaultRemoteProxy",
     "maxSession": 2,
     "hubHost": "192.168.1.100",
     "role": "webdriver",
     "registerCycle": 5000,
     "hub": "http://192.168.1.100:4444/grid/register",
     "hubPort": 4444,
     "remoteHost": "http://192.168.1.102:5555"
    }
}
```

We can now pass the `selenium-node-win-ie10.cfg.json` configuration file through command-line arguments as follows:

```
java -Dwebdriver.ie.driver="C:\SeDrivers\IEDriverServer.exe"-jar
selenium-server-standalone-2.41.0.jar -role webdriver -nodeConfig
selenium-node-win-ie10.cfg.json
```

Adding a Firefox node

To add a Firefox node, open a new command prompt or terminal window and navigate to the location where the Selenium server JAR is located. To launch and add a node to the Grid, type the following command:

```
java -jar selenium-server-standalone-2.41.0.jar -role webdriver -browser
"browserName=firefox,version=27,maxinstance=2,platform=WINDOWS" -hubHost
localhost -port 6666
```

In this example, we set `maxinstance` to 2. This tells Grid that this node will support two instances of Firefox. Once the node has started, the following configuration will appear in Grid console:

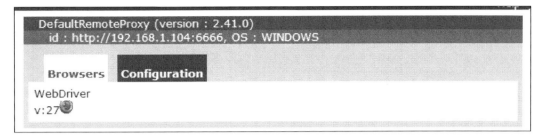

Adding a Chrome node

To add Chrome node, open a new command prompt or terminal window and navigate to the location where the Selenium server JAR is located. To launch and add the node to the Grid, type following command:

```
java -Dwebdriver.chrome.driver="C:\SeDrivers\chromedriver.exe" -jar
selenium-server-standalone-2.41.0.jar -role webdriver -browser "browserN
ame=chrome,version=35,maxinstance=2,platform=WINDOWS" -hubHost localhost
-port 7777
```

Once the node has started, the following configuration will appear in the Grid console:

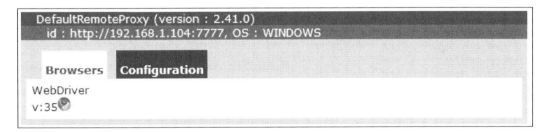

Mac OS X with Safari

We added IE, Firefox, and Chrome instances from a Windows machine, now let's add a Safari node from a Mac OS. Open a new terminal window and navigate to the location where the Selenium server JAR is located. To launch and add the node to the Grid type the following command:

```
java -jar selenium-server-standalone-2.41.0.jar -role webdriver -browser
"browserName=safari,version=7,maxinstance=1,platform=MAC" -hubHost
192.168.1.104 -port 8888
```

Once the node has started, the following configuration will appear on the Grid console:

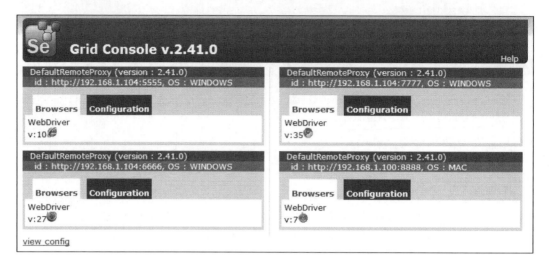

Now, we have our Selenium Grid set up, let's try running tests on this Grid.

Running tests in Grid

Running tests in Grid and with different combinations of browsers and operating systems will need a few tweaks to the tests that we created earlier. We specified hardcoded browser and platform names in the desired capabilities. If we hardcode the values, then we will end up having a separate script for each combination. To avoid this and use a single test that will work on all the combinations, we need to parameterize the browser and platform values passed to the desired capabilities class as given in the following steps:

1. We will pass the browser and platform to the tests from the command line. For example, if we want to run test on the Windows and Chrome combination we will run the script through the command line in the following way:

    ```
    python grid_test.py WINDOWS chrome
    ```

2. If we want to run tests on Safari on Mac, we can use following command:

    ```
    python grid_test.py MAC safari
    ```

3. To implement this, we need to add two global attributes, PLATFORM and BROWSER, to the test class in the following way. We will set a default value in case values are not supplied from the command line:

```
class SearchProducts(unittest.TestCase):

    PLATFORM = 'WINDOWS'
    BROWSER = 'firefox'
```

4. Next we need to parameterize the desired capabilities in the setUp() method as shown in the following code:

```
desired_caps = {}
desired_caps['platform'] = self.PLATFORM
desired_caps['browserName'] = self.BROWSER
```

5. Finally, we need to read the arguments passed to the script and assign the values to the PLATFORM and BROWSER attributes in the following way:

```
if __name__ == '__main__':
    if len(sys.argv) > 1:
        SearchProducts.BROWSER = sys.argv.pop()
        SearchProducts.PLATFORM = sys.argv.pop()
    unittest.main()
```

6. That's it. Our test is now ready to handle any given combination. Here is the complete code with the previous changes:

```
import sys
import unittest
from selenium import webdriver

class SearchProducts(unittest.TestCase):

    PLATFORM = 'WINDOWS'
    BROWSER = 'firefox'

    def setUp(self):

        desired_caps = {}
        desired_caps['platform'] = self.PLATFORM
        desired_caps['browserName'] = self.BROWSER

        self.driver = \
            webdriver.Remote('http://192.168.1.104:4444/wd/hub',
            desired_caps)
        self.driver.get('http://demo.magentocommerce.com/')
        self.driver.implicitly_wait(30)
        self.driver.maximize_window()
```

```
        def testSearchByCategory(self):

            # get the search textbox
            self.search_field = self.driver.find_element_by_name('q')
            self.search_field.clear()

            # enter search keyword and submit
            self.search_field.send_keys('phones')
            self.search_field.submit()

            # get all the anchor elements which have product names
            # displayed currently on result page using
            # find_elements_by_xpath method
            products = self.driver.\
                find_elements_by_xpath('//h2[@class=\'product-
                name\']/a')

            # check count of products shown in results
            self.assertEqual(2, len(products))

        def tearDown(self):
            # close the browser window
            self.driver.quit()

if __name__ == '__main__':
    if len(sys.argv) > 1:
        SearchProducts.BROWSER = sys.argv.pop()
        SearchProducts.PLATFORM = sys.argv.pop()
    unittest.main(verbosity=2)
```

7. To run the test, open a new command prompt or terminal window and navigate to the location of the script. Type the following command and you will see that the Grid will connect the node matching with the given platform and browser and execute the test on that node:

```
python grid_test.py MAC safari
```

Running tests in a cloud

We set up a local grid in the previous steps to run the tests for cross-browser testing. This requires setting up physical or virtual machines with different browsers and operating systems. There are costs and efforts needed to get the required hardware, software, and support to run the test lab. You also need to put in efforts to keep this infrastructure updated with the latest versions and patches, and so on. Not everybody can afford these costs and efforts.

Instead of investing and setting up a cross-browser test lab, you can easily outsource a virtual test lab to a third-party cloud provider. Sauce Labs and BrowserStack are leading cloud-based cross-browser testing cloud providers. Both of these have support for over 400 different browser and operating system configurations including mobile and tablet devices and support running Selenium WebDriver tests in their cloud.

In this section, we will set up and run a test in Sauce Labs cloud. The steps are similar if you want to run tests with BrowserStack.

Using Sauce Labs

Let's set up and run a test with Sauce Labs using the following steps:

1. You need a free Sauce Labs account to begin with. Register for a free account on Sauce Labs at `https://saucelabs.com/` and get the username and access key. Sauce Labs provides all the required hardware and software infrastructure to run your tests in the cloud.

2. You can get the access key from the Sauce Labs dashboard after login as shown:

3. Let's modify the test we created earlier to run with Grid and add steps to run this test on Sauce Labs cloud.

4. We need to add the Sauce username and access key to the test and change the Grid address to Sauce's Grid address passing the username and access key as shown in the following code:

```
import sys
import unittest
from selenium import webdriver


class SearchProducts(unittest.TestCase):

    PLATFORM = 'WINDOWS'
    BROWSER = 'phantomjs'
    SAUCE_USERNAME = 'upgundecha'
```

```
    SUACE_KEY = 'c6e7132c-ae27-4217-b6fa-3cf7df0a7281'

def setUp(self):

    desired_caps = {}
    desired_caps['platform'] = self.PLATFORM
    desired_caps['browserName'] = self.BROWSER

    sauce_string = self.SAUCE_USERNAME + ':' + self.SUACE_KEY

    self.driver = \
        webdriver.Remote('http://' + sauce_string +
        '@ondemand.saucelabs.com:80/wd/hub', desired_caps)
    self.driver.get('http://demo.magentocommerce.com/')
    self.driver.implicitly_wait(30)
    self.driver.maximize_window()

def testSearchByCategory(self):

    # get the search textbox
    self.search_field = self.driver.find_element_by_name('q')
    self.search_field.clear()

    # enter search keyword and submit
    self.search_field.send_keys('phones')
    self.search_field.submit()

    # get all the anchor elements which have product names
    # displayed currently on result page using
    # find_elements_by_xpath method
    products = self.driver.\
        find_elements_by_xpath('//h2[@class=\'product-
        name\']/a')

    # check count of products shown in results
    self.assertEqual(2, len(products))

def tearDown(self):
    # close the browser window
    self.driver.quit()

if __name__ == '__main__':
    if len(sys.argv) > 1:
        SearchProducts.BROWSER = sys.argv.pop()
        SearchProducts.PLATFORM = sys.argv.pop()
    unittest.main(verbosity=2)
```

5. To run the test, open a new command prompt or terminal window and navigate to the location of the script. Type following command:

```
python sauce_test.py "OS X 10.9" "Safari"
```

You can get a list of Platforms supported on Sauce Labs at `https://saucelabs.com/platforms`.

While running the test, it will connect to Sauce Lab's grid server and request for the desired operating system and browser configuration. Sauce assigns a virtual machine for our test to run on the given configuration.

6. We can monitor this run on Sauce dashboard as shown in the following screenshot:

We can further drill down on the Sauce session and see exactly what happened during the run. It provides a lot of details including the Selenium commands, screenshots, Selenium logs, and video of the execution as shown in the following screenshot:

 You can also test the application securely hosted on the internal servers by using the Sauce Connect utility that creates a secure tunnel between your machine and the Sauce cloud.

Summary

In this chapter, you learned how to run tests on remote machines with the Selenium standalone server. The Selenium standalone server enables us to run tests on remote machines for testing our application against a combination of browsers and operating systems for cross-browser testing. This increases coverage for testing and making sure applications run on the desired combinations.

We then looked at setting up Selenium Grid to run tests in a distributed architecture. Selenium Grid removes complexity in performing cross-browser testing by providing a transparent execution against multiple machines. It also brings down the time to run the tests.

We also looked at using a cloud-based, cross-browser testing provider. We executed a test on Sauce Labs. This offers all the necessary test infrastructure to run the tests on hundreds of different combinations with minimal costs.

In the next chapter, you will learn how to test mobile applications using Appium and Selenium WebDriver, using some of the concepts you learned in this chapter. Appium supports testing native, hybrid, and web mobile applications on iOS and Android. We will set up Appium and run tests against the mobile version of the sample application.

7
Testing on Mobile

With the ever increasing number of mobile users all over the world, the adoption of smartphones and tablets has increased quite significantly. Mobile apps have penetrated consumer and enterprise markets replacing desktops and laptops with smart devices. Small businesses and large-scale enterprises have a great potential to use mobile as a channel to connect with users. There is a lot of effort being taken to build mobile-friendly websites and native applications to serve customers and employees. Testing these apps on various mobile platforms available in the market has become crucial. This chapter will teach you more on how to test mobile apps using Selenium WebDriver and more specifically using **Appium**.

In this chapter, you will learn about:

- Testing mobile apps with Appium
- Installing and setting up Appium
- Creating and running tests for iOS on iPhone simulator
- Creating and running tests for Android on a real device

Introducing Appium

Appium is an open source test automation framework for testing native and hybrid mobile apps on iOS, Android, and Firefox OS platforms using the JSON wire protocol used by the Selenium WebDriver tests to communicate with the Selenium Server. Appium will replace the `iPhoneDriver` and `AndroidDriver` APIs in Selenium 2 used for testing mobile web applications.

Appium allows us to use and extend the existing Selenium WebDriver framework to build mobile tests. As it uses Selenium WebDriver to drive the tests, we can use any language to create tests for which the Selenium client library exists. Here is the Appium coverage map with support for different platforms and application types:

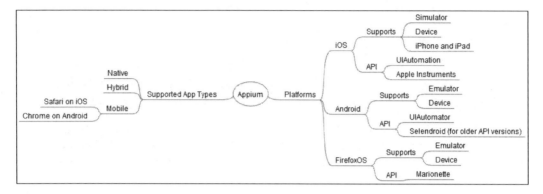

Appium supports testing of the following types of apps:

- **Native apps**: Native apps are platform-specific apps built using the platform-supported languages and frameworks. For example, apps for iPhone and iPad are developed using Objective-C with iOS SDK; similarly, Android apps are developed using Java with Android SDK. In terms of performance, native apps are fast and more reliable. They use the native framework for the user interface.

- **Mobile web apps**: Mobile web apps are server-side apps, built with any server-side technology such as PHP, Java, or ASP.NET, and use frameworks such as jQuery Mobile, Sencha Touch, and so on to render a user interface that mimics the native UI.

- **Hybrid apps**: Similar to the native apps, hybrid apps run on the device and are written with web technologies (HTML5, CSS, and JavaScript). Hybrid apps use the device's browser engine to render the HTML and process the JavaScript locally inside a native container using WebView. This enables the app to access device capabilities that are not accessible in mobile web apps, such as the camera, accelerometer, sensors, and local storage.

Prerequisites for Appium

Before you get started with learning more about Appium, you will need some tools for iOS and Android platforms.

Appium is built on Node.js and comes as a Node.js package as well as standalone GUI on Mac OS X and Windows. We will use Appium standalone GUI which comes with built-in Node.js on Mac OS X.

Setting up Xcode for iOS

We need Xcode 4.6.3 or higher, installed on Mac OS X, for testing apps for the iOS platform. While writing this book, Xcode 5.1 was used. You can get Xcode from the App Store or developer portal at `https://developer.apple.com/xcode/`.

After installing Xcode, launch it from the **Applications** menu and navigate to **Preferences** | **Downloads**, and install **Command Line Tools** and additional iOS SDKs for testing applications on different versions of the iOS platform, as shown in the following screenshot:

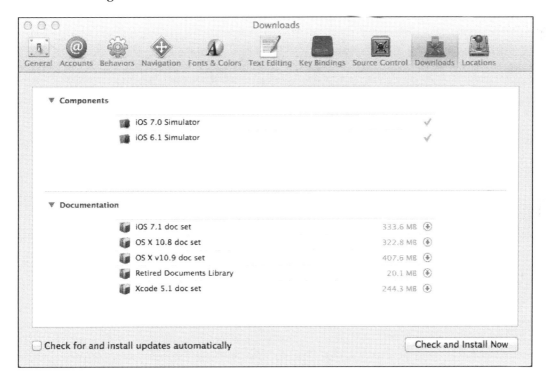

For running tests on a real device, you need a provision profile installed on the device and USB debugging enabled on it.

Try to launch the iPhone simulator and verify that it works. You can launch the simulator by navigating to **Xcode | Open Developer Tool | iOS Simulator**. Launch Safari in the simulator and open the mobile web app version of the sample application `http://demo.magentocommerce.com` in Safari as shown in the following screenshot:

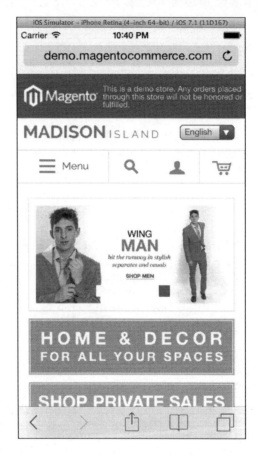

Setting up Android SDK

We will need the Android SDK installed for testing Android apps. Android SDK is available for download at `http://developer.android.com/sdk/`. This will get us the latest version of the SDK. After the installation, please make sure `ANDROID_HOME` is added to the path. Complete installation steps are available at `http://developer.android.com/sdk/installing/index.html?pkg=tools`.

 For detailed and latest installation requirements visit `http://appium.io/getting-started.html#requirements`.

Setting up the Appium Python client package

The Appium Python client was fully compliant with the Selenium 3.0 specification draft at the time of writing this book. It offers some helpers to make mobile testing in Python easier with Appium. This can be installed using the following command:

```
pip install Appium-Python-Client
```

> More information on the Appium Python client package is available at https://pypi.python.org/pypi/Appium-Python-Client.

Installing Appium

Before we start testing mobile apps with Appium, we need to download and install Appium. We will use the Appium GUI version. If you wish to run tests for iOS on iPhone or iPad, then you need to set up Appium on a Mac OS X machine. For testing Android applications, you can set up the environment on a Windows or Linux machine. Setting up Appium is fairly easy with the new Appium app for Mac OS X. You can download the latest Appium binaries from http://appium.io/. Follow the given steps to install Appium:

1. Click on the **Download Appium** button on the front page and you will be directed to the download page.

2. Select the version specific to the operating system you are using from the list as shown in the following screenshot:

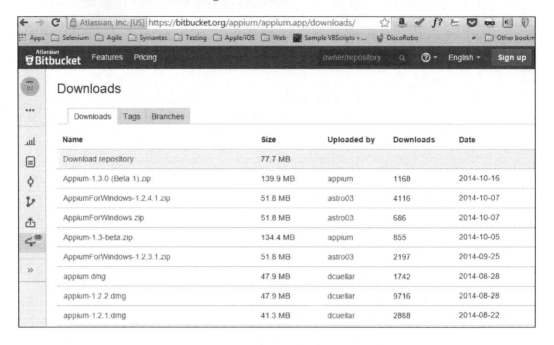

 In the following examples, we will be using Appium on Mac OS X.

3. You can install Appium on Mac by launching the installer and copying Appium to the `Applications` folder.

When you launch Appium from the `Applications` menu for the first time, it will ask for authorization to run the iOS simulators.

 By default, Appium starts at `http://127.0.0.1:4723` or localhost. This is the URL to which your test should direct the test commands. We will be testing the mobile version of the sample application that we used in the book on iPhone Safari browser.

4. On the main window of Appium, click on the Apple icon to open iOS settings:

5. On the **iOS Settings** dialog, select the **Force Device** checkbox and specify **iPhone 4s** in the iOS section. Also, select the **Use Mobile Safari** checkbox as shown in the following screenshot:

6. Click on the **Launch** button in the Appium window to start the Appium server.

Appium Inspector

Appium also comes with a spy tool called **Appium Inspector**. We can launch the Appium Inspector by clicking on the magnifying glass icon on Appium's main window.

The Inspector provides a lot of options to analyze the app under test. One of the main features it offers is how the UI elements are used in the app, the structure or hierarchy of the elements, and the properties of these elements, which we can use in defining the locator strings.

You can also simulate various gestures on the app and see their effect on the simulator. It also offers an ability to record the steps you perform on the app.

Testing on iOS

Appium drives automation using various native automation frameworks and provides an API based on Selenium's WebDriver JSON wire protocol. For automating iOS applications, it uses the UI Automation feature offered as part of Apple Instruments.

Appium works as an HTTP server and receives the commands from test scripts over the JSON wire protocol. Appium sends these commands to Apple Instruments so that the commands can be executed on the app launched in a simulator or real device. While doing so, Appium translates the JSON commands into UI Automation JavaScript commands that are understood by the Instruments. The Instruments take care of launching and closing the app in the simulator or device. This process is shown in the following diagram:

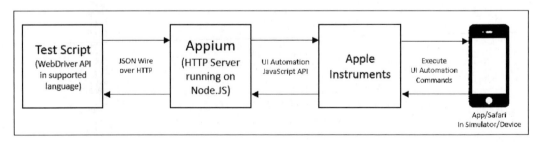

When a command is executed against the app on the simulator or device, the target app sends the response back to the Instruments, which then sends it back to Appium in the JavaScript response format. Appium translates the UI Automation JavaScript responses into Selenium WebDriver JSON wire protocol responses and sends them back to the test script.

Writing a test for iOS

Now, we have the Appium running; let's create a test that will check the search functionality in the iPhone Safari browser. Create a new test, SearchProductsOnIPhone, with the following code:

```
import unittest
from appium import webdriver


class SearchProductsOnIPhone(unittest.TestCase):
    def setUp(self):
        desired_caps = {}
        # platform
        desired_caps['device'] = 'iPhone Simulator'
        # platform version
        desired_caps['version'] = '7.1'
        # mobile browser
        desired_caps['app'] = 'safari'

        # to connect to Appium server use RemoteWebDriver
        # and pass desired capabilities
        self.driver = \
            webdriver.Remote("http://127.0.0.1:4723/wd/hub"
              , desired_caps)
        self.driver.get("http://demo.magentocommerce.com/")
        self.driver.implicitly_wait(30)
        self.driver.maximize_window()

    def test_search_by_category(self):

        # click on search icon
        self.driver.find_element_by_xpath
          ("//a[@href='#header-search']").click()
        # get the search textbox
        self.search_field = self.driver.find_element_by_name("q")
        self.search_field.clear()
```

```
        # enter search keyword and submit
        self.search_field.send_keys("phones")
        self.search_field.submit()

        # get all the anchor elements which have product names
        # displayed currently on result page using
        # find_elements_by_xpath method
        products = self.driver\
            .find_elements_by_xpath
              ("//div[@class='category-products']/ul/li")

        # check count of products shown in results
        self.assertEqual(2, len(products))

    def tearDown(self):
        # close the browser window
        self.driver.quit()

if __name__ == '__main__':
    unittest.main(verbosity=2)
```

We need `RemoteWebDriver` to run the tests with Appium. However, for Appium to use the desired platform, we need to pass a set of desired capabilities as shown in the following code:

```
desired_caps = {}
# platform
desired_caps['device'] = 'iPhone Simulator'
# platform version
desired_caps['version'] = '7.1'
# mobile browser
desired_caps['app'] = 'safari'
```

The `desired_caps['device']` capability is used by Appium to decide on which the platform the test script should get executed. In this example, we used `iPhone Simulator`. For running tests on iPad, we can specify the iPad Simulator.

When running tests on a real device, we need to specify the value `iPhone` or `iPad` for device capability. Appium will pick the device that is connected to the Mac via USB.

The `desired_caps['version']` capability is the version of iPhone/iPad simulator that we want to use. In this example, iOS 7.1 simulator is used, which was the latest the version of iOS at the time of writing this book.

The last desired capability we used is `desired_caps['app']`, which is used by Appium to launch the target app. In this case, it will launch the Safari browser.

Finally, we need to connect to the Appium server using `RemoteWebDriver` and the desired capabilities that we need. This is done by creating an instance of `Remote` as shown in following code:

```
self.driver = webdriver.Remote
    ("http://127.0.0.1:4723/wd/hub", desired_caps)
```

The rest of the test uses the Selenium API to interact with the mobile web version of the application. Run the test normally. You will see that Appium establishes a session with test scripts and launches the iPhone Simulator with the Safari app. Appium will execute all the test steps by running commands on the Safari app in the simulator window.

Testing on Android

Appium drives the automation of Android applications using the UI Automator bundled with Android SDK. The process is quite similar to testing on iOS.

Appium works as an HTTP server and receives the commands from test scripts over JSON wire protocol. Appium sends these commands to the UI Automator so that they can be executed on the app launched in an emulator or real device. While doing so, Appium translates the JSON commands into the UI Automator Java commands that are understood by Android SDK. This process is shown in the following diagram:

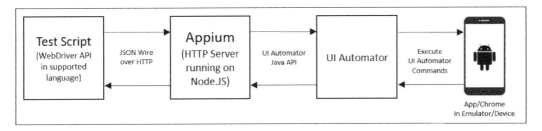

When a command is executed against the app on the emulator or device, the target app sends the response back to the UI Automator, which sends it back to Appium. It translates the UI Automator responses into Selenium WebDriver JSON wire protocol responses and sends them back to the test script.

Writing a test for Android

Testing apps on Android is pretty much similar to what we did for iOS. For Android, we will use a real device instead of an emulator (a simulator is called an emulator in the Android community). We will use the same application for testing in Chrome for Android.

For this example, I am using Samsung Galaxy S III handset. We need to install the Chrome browser on the device. You can get Google Chrome on the Play Store. Next, we need to connect the device to the machine where the Appium server is running.

Now, we will work on Android. Here, we will try to execute our test scripts on the Android real device. We need to make sure we have installed Chrome on our Android device and connect our device to our machine. Let's run the following command to get a list of emulators or devices connected to the machine:

```
./adb devices
```

Android Debug Bridge (adb) is a command-line tool available in Android SDK that lets you communicate with an emulator instance or the connected real device.

The previous command will display a list of all the Android devices that are connected to the host. In this example, we have connected to a real device that is listed as shown in the following screenshot:

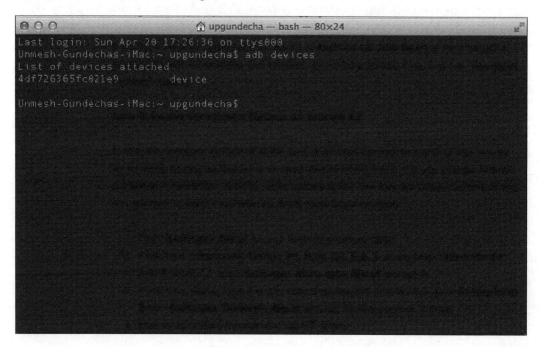

Let's use the test that we created for iOS and modify it for Android. We will create a new test, SearchProductsOnAndroid. Copy the following code to the newly created test:

```
import unittest
from appium import webdriver


class SearchProductsOnAndroid(unittest.TestCase):
    def setUp(self):
        desired_caps = {}
        # platform
        desired_caps['device'] = 'Android'
        # platform version
        desired_caps['version'] = '4.3'
        # mobile browser
        desired_caps['app'] = 'Chrome'

        # to connect to Appium server use RemoteWebDriver
        # and pass desired capabilities
        self.driver = \
            webdriver.Remote("http://127.0.0.1:4723/wd
                /hub", desired_caps)
        self.driver.get("http://demo.magentocommerce.com/")
        self.driver.implicitly_wait(30)

    def test_search_by_category(self):

        # click on search icon
        self.driver.find_element_by_xpath
          ("//a[@href='#header-search']").click()
        # get the search textbox
        self.search_field = self.driver.find_element_by_name("q")
        self.search_field.clear()

        # enter search keyword and submit
        self.search_field.send_keys("phones")
        self.search_field.submit()

        # get all the anchor elements which have product names
        # displayed currently on result page using
        # find_elements_by_xpath method
        products = self.driver\
```

```
            .find_elements_by_xpath
                ("//div[@class='category-products']/ul/li")

        # check count of products shown in results
        self.assertEqual(2, len(products))

    def tearDown(self):
        # close the browser window
        self.driver.quit()

if __name__ == '__main__':
    unittest.main(verbosity=2)
```

In this example, we assigned the `desired_caps['device']` capability value to Android, which will be used by the Appium to run tests on Android.

Next, we mentioned the Android Version 4.3 (Jelly Bean) in the `desired_caps['version']` capability. As we want to run tests in Chrome for Android, we mentioned Chrome in the `desired_caps['app']` capability.

Appium will use the first device from the list of devices that adb returns. It will use the desired capabilities that we mentioned, launch the Chrome browser on the device, and start executing the test script commands, as shown in the following screenshot:

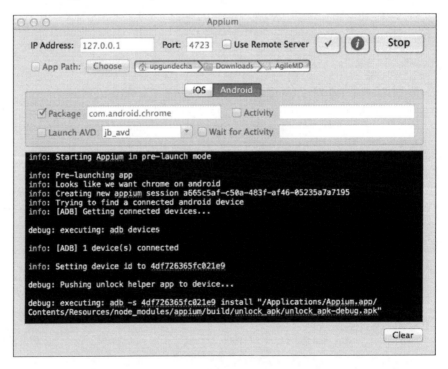

Here is the screenshot of the test running on a real device:

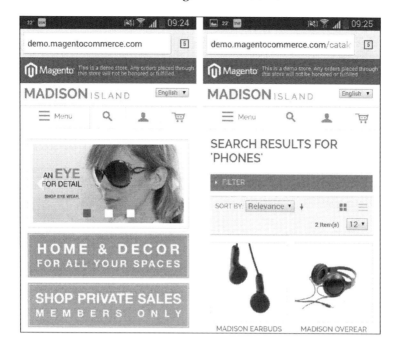

Using Sauce Labs

We looked at Sauce Labs for cross-browser testing in *Chapter 6, Cross-browser Testing*. Sauce also provides support for testing mobile applications using Appium. In fact, the Appium project is developed and supported by Sauce Labs. With minimal changes to the desired capabilities, we can run mobile tests in Sauce Labs with the following code:

```
import unittest
from appium import webdriver


class SearchProductsOnIPhone(unittest.TestCase):
    SAUCE_USERNAME = 'upgundecha'
    SUACE_KEY = 'c6e7132c-ae27-4217-b6fa-3cf7df0a7281'

    def setUp(self):

        desired_caps = {}
        desired_caps['browserName'] = "Safari"
```

```
            desired_caps['platformVersion'] = "7.1"
            desired_caps['platformName'] = "iOS"
            desired_caps['deviceName'] = "iPhone Simulator"

            sauce_string = self.SAUCE_USERNAME + ':' + self.SUACE_KEY

            self.driver = \
                webdriver.Remote('http://' + sauce_string +
                    '@ondemand.saucelabs.com:80/wd/hub', desired_caps)
            self.driver.get('http://demo.magentocommerce.com/')
            self.driver.implicitly_wait(30)
            self.driver.maximize_window()

        def test_search_by_category(self):
            # click on search icon
            self.driver.find_element_by_xpath("//a[@href=
                '#header-search']").click()
            # get the search textbox
            self.search_field = self.driver.find_element_by_name("q")
            self.search_field.clear()

            # enter search keyword and submit
            self.search_field.send_keys("phones")
            self.search_field.submit()

            # get all the anchor elements which have
            # product names displayed
            # currently on result page using
            # find_elements_by_xpath method
            products = self.driver\
                .find_elements_by_xpath
                    ("//div[@class='category-products']/ul/li")

            # check count of products shown in results
            self.assertEqual(2, len(products))

        def tearDown(self):
            # close the browser window
            self.driver.quit()

    if __name__ == '__main__':
        unittest.main(verbosity=2)
```

After running the mobile tests, we can see the results and video recording in the Sauce Labs dashboard. This saves a lot of effort and time in setting up Appium in the local environment with Sauce offering various combinations of SDKs and settings.

Summary

In this chapter, we recognized the need for testing apps on mobile devices. We looked at Appium, which is becoming a core feature of Selenium for testing mobile apps. We installed and set up Appium for testing a mobile version of the sample app.

We tested the mobile web application on the iPhone simulator and on the Android device. Using Appium, we can test various types of mobile applications and use any programming language that has a `WebDriver` client library.

In the next chapter, you will learn some good practices such as using `PageObjects` and data-driven tests with Selenium WebDriver.

8
Page Objects and Data-driven Testing

This chapter introduces two important design patterns that are useful in creating scalable and maintainable test automation framework designs. We will explore how to use the data-driven approach to create data-driven Selenium tests using Python libraries.

In the second part of this chapter, you will learn about using the page object pattern to create highly maintainable and robust tests by separating locators and other low-level calls from the test cases into a layer of abstraction, which resembles the functionality of the application similar to what the user experiences within the browser window.

In this chapter, you will learn:

- What data-driven testing is
- How to use the **Data-driven testing (ddt)** library along with the `unittest` library to create data-driven tests
- How to read data from external sources for data-driven testing
- What the page object pattern is and how it helps in creating a maintainable test suite
- How to implement the page object pattern for the sample application

Data-driven testing

By using the data-driven testing approach, we can use a single test to verify different sets of test cases or test data by driving the test with input and expected values from an external data source instead of using the hardcoded values every time a test is run.

This becomes useful when we have similar tests that consist of the same steps but differ in the input data and expected value or the application state. Here is an example of a set of login test cases with different combinations:

Description	Test data	Expected output
Valid username and password	A pair of valid usernames and passwords	The user should log in to the application with a success message
Invalid username and password	An invalid username and password	The user should be displayed the login error
Valid username and invalid password	A valid username and an invalid password	The user should be displayed the login error

We can create a single script that can handle the test data and the conditions from the preceding table.

By using the data-driven testing approach, we separate the test data from the test logic by replacing the hardcoded test data with variables using the data from external sources such as CSV or a spreadsheet file. This also helps in creating reusable tests that can run with different sets of data, which can be kept outside of the test.

Data-driven testing also helps in increasing the test coverage as we can handle multiple test conditions while minimizing the amount of test code we need to write and maintain.

In this section, we will implement the data-driven testing approach to some of the tests that we created in the earlier chapters, using the ddt library in Python.

Using ddt for data-driven tests

The ddt library provides the ability to parameterize the test cases written using the unittest library in Python. We can provide a set of data using ddt to a test case for data-driven tests.

The ddt library provides a set of class and method decorators that we can use to create data-driven tests.

Installing ddt

We can download and install ddt using the following command line:

```
pip install ddt
```

That's it! You can find more about ddt at https://pypi.python.org/pypi/ddt.

Creating a simple data-driven test with ddt in unittest

We will use the search test case on the sample application and convert it into a data-driven test by removing the hardcoded values to search for different products and categories.

To create a data-driven test we need to use the @ddt decorator for the test class and use the @data decorator on the data-driven test methods.

The @data decorator takes as many arguments as we have values that we want to feed to the test. These could be single values or lists, tuples, and dictionaries. For lists, we need to use the @unpack decorator, which unpacks tuples or lists into multiple arguments.

Let's implement the search test, which accepts a pair of arguments for different search terms and expected result count as shown in the following code:

```python
import unittest
from ddt import ddt, data, unpack
from selenium import webdriver

@ddt
class SearchDDT(unittest.TestCase):
    def setUp(self):
        # create a new Firefox session
        self.driver = webdriver.Firefox()
        self.driver.implicitly_wait(30)
        self.driver.maximize_window()

        # navigate to the application home page
        self.driver.get("http://demo.magentocommerce.com/")

    # specify test data using @data decorator
    @data(("phones", 2), ("music", 5))
    @unpack
    def test_search(self, search_value, expected_count):
        # get the search textbox
        self.search_field = self.driver.find_element_by_name("q")
        self.search_field.clear()
```

```
            # enter search keyword and submit.
            # use search_value argument to pass data
            self.search_field.send_keys(search_value)
            self.search_field.submit()

            # get all the anchor elements which have
            # product names displayed
            # currently on result page using
            # find_elements_by_xpath method
            products = self.driver.find_elements_by_xpath
                ("//h2[@class='product-name']/a")

            # check count of products shown in results
            self.assertEqual(expected_count, len(products))

        def tearDown(self):
            # close the browser window
            self.driver.quit()

    if __name__ == '__main__':
        unittest.main(verbosity=2)
```

In this test, we are passing a list of tuples using the `@data` decorator. The `@unpack` decorator is used to unpack these tuples into multiple arguments. The `test_search()` method accepts the `search_value` and `expected_count` arguments, which will be mapped to the tuple values by `ddt`, as shown:

```
    # specify test data using @data decorator
        @data(("phones", 2), ("music", 5))
        @unpack
        def test_search(self, search_value, expected_count):
```

When we run the test, `ddt` will generate new test methods giving them meaningful names by converting the data values to valid Python identifiers. For example, for the preceding test, `ddt` will generate new test methods with names as shown in the following screenshot:

Using external data sources for data-driven tests

In the previous example, we supplied the test data in the test code. However, you will find situations where you already have test data defined in external sources such as text files, spreadsheets, or databases. It is also a good idea to separate the test data from the code and put it in an external source for easy maintenance and avoid changes to the test code each time you want to update the values.

Let's explore how we can read the test data from the **Comma separated values (CSV)** files or Excel spreadsheets and supply it to `ddt`.

Reading values from CSV

We will use the previous test case and move the data that we supplied to the `@data` decorator into a separate CSV file called `testdata.csv` instead of keeping it in the script. This data will be stored in a tabular format as shown in the following screenshot:

Next, we will implement the `get_data()` method, which accepts the path and name of the CSV file. This method uses the `csv` library to read the values from the file and returns a list of these values. We will use the `get_data()` method in the `@data` decorator as shown in the following code:

```python
import csv, unittest
from ddt import ddt, data, unpack
from selenium import webdriver


def get_data(file_name):
    # create an empty list to store rows
    rows = []
```

```
        # open the CSV file
        data_file = open(file_name, "rb")
        # create a CSV Reader from CSV file
        reader = csv.reader(data_file)
        # skip the headers
        next(reader, None)
        # add rows from reader to list
        for row in reader:
            rows.append(row)
        return rows


@ddt
class SearchCsvDDT(unittest.TestCase):
    def setUp(self):
        # create a new Firefox session
        self.driver = webdriver.Firefox()
        self.driver.implicitly_wait(30)
        self.driver.maximize_window()

        # navigate to the application home page
        self.driver.get("http://demo.magentocommerce.com/")

    # get the data from specified csv file by
    # calling the get_data function
    @data(*get_data("testdata.csv"))
    @unpack
    def test_search(self, search_value, expected_count):
            self.search_field =
              self.driver.find_element_by_name("q")
            self.search_field.clear()

            # enter search keyword and submit.
            self.search_field.send_keys(search_value)
            self.search_field.submit()

            # get all the anchor elements which have
            # product names displayed
            # currently on result page using
            # find_elements_by_xpath method
            products = self.driver.find_elements_by_xpath
              ("//h2[@class='product-name']/a")
            expected_count = int(expected_count)
            if expected_count > 0:
                # check count of products shown in results
```

```
                    self.assertEqual(expected_count, len(products))
                else:
                    msg = self.driver.find_element_by_class_name
                      ("note-msg")
                    self.assertEqual
                      ("Your search returns no results.", msg.text)

        def tearDown(self):
            # close the browser window
            self.driver.quit()

    if __name__ == '__main__':
        unittest.main()
```

When this test is executed, @data will call the get_data() method, which will read the supplied file and return the list of values back to @data. These values are unpacked and the test methods are generated for each row.

Reading values from Excel

Maintaining test data in the Excel spreadsheet is another common practice. It also helps nontechnical users to define new tests by simply adding a row of data in a spreadsheet. Consider the following screenshot as an example of maintaining the data in an Excel spreadsheet:

A	B
Category/Product	NumberOfProducts
phones	2
music	5
iphone 5s	0

Reading values from the Excel spreadsheet will need another library called xlrd, which can be installed with the following command:

```
pip install xlrd
```

The `xlrd` library provides read access to the workbook, sheet, and cells in order to read the data. It does not write to a spreadsheet. For writing the data, we can use the `xlwt` library. We can also use `openpyxl` for reading and writing data in a spreadsheet. Find more information at `http://www.python-excel.org/`.

Let's modify the `get_data()` method from the previous example to read data from a spreadsheet into a list and modify the test as shown in the following code:

```python
import xlrd, unittest
from ddt import ddt, data, unpack
from selenium import webdriver

def get_data(file_name):
    # create an empty list to store rows
    rows = []
    # open the specified Excel spreadsheet as workbook
    book = xlrd.open_workbook(file_name)
    # get the first sheet
    sheet = book.sheet_by_index(0)
    # iterate through the sheet and get data from rows in list
    for row_idx in range(1, sheet.nrows):
        rows.append(list(sheet.row_values(row_idx, 0, sheet.ncols)))
    return rows

@ddt
class SearchExcelDDT(unittest.TestCase):
    def setUp(self):
        # create a new Firefox session
        self.driver = webdriver.Firefox()
        self.driver.implicitly_wait(30)
        self.driver.maximize_window()

        # navigate to the application home page
        self.driver.get("http://demo.magentocommerce.com/")

    # get the data from specified Excel spreadsheet
    # by calling the get_data function
    @data(*get_data("TestData.xlsx"))
    @unpack
    def test_search(self, search_value, expected_count):
            self.search_field = \
                self.driver.find_element_by_name("q")
```

```
        self.search_field.clear()

        # enter search keyword and submit.
        self.search_field.send_keys(search_value)
        self.search_field.submit()

        # get all the anchor elements which have
        # product names displayed
        # currently on result page using
        # find_elements_by_xpath method
        products = self.driver.find_elements_by_xpath
            ("//h2[@class='product-name']/a")
        if expected_count > 0:
            # check count of products shown in results
            self.assertEqual(expected_count, len(products))
        else:
            msg = self.driver.
                find_element_by_class_name("note-msg")
            self.assertEqual("Your search returns
                no results.", msg.text)

    def tearDown(self):
        # close the browser window
        self.driver.quit()

if __name__ == '__main__':
    unittest.main()
```

Similar to the previous example for CSV files, when this test is executed @data will call the get_data() method, which will read the supplied file and return the list of values back to @data from a spreadsheet. These values are unpacked and the test methods are generated for each row.

Reading values from a database

If you need to read values from a database, you just need to modify the get_data() method and use the appropriate libraries to connect to the database and read values using SQL queries back into a list.

The page objects pattern

Until now, we were writing Selenium WebDriver tests directly into Python classes using `unittest`. We were specifying locators and test case steps into these classes. This code is good to start; however, as we progress on, adding more and more tests to our tests suite, it will become difficult to maintain. This will make tests brittle.

Developing maintainable and reusable test code is important for sustainable test automation and the test code should be treated as production code and similar standards and patterns should to be applied while developing the test code.

To overcome these problems, we can use various design patterns and principles such as **Don't Repeat Yourself (DRY)**, and code refactoring techniques while creating the tests. If you're a developer, you might already be using these techniques.

The page object pattern is one of the highly used patterns among the Selenium user community to structure the tests, making them separate from low-level actions, and providing a high-level abstraction. You can compare the page object pattern to the facade pattern, which enables creating a simplified interface for complex code.

The page object pattern offers creating an object representing each web page from the application under test. We can define classes for each page, modeling all attributes and actions for that page. This creates a layer of separation between the test code and technical implementation of pages and application functionality that we will be testing, by hiding the locators, low-level methods dealing with elements, and business functionality. Instead, the page objects will provide a high-level API for tests to deal with the page functionality.

Tests should use these page objects at a high level, where any change in attributes or actions in the underlying page should not break the test. Using the page object pattern provides the following benefits:

- Creating a high-level abstraction that helps minimize changes when the underlying page is modified by developers. So, you will change only the page object and the calling tests will be unaffected.
- Creating reusable code that can be shared across multiple test cases.
- Tests are more readable, flexible, and maintainable.

Let's start refactoring the test that we created in the earlier chapter and implement the page objects that provide a high-level abstraction for the application that we are testing. In this example, we will create the following structure for the selected pages in the sample application. We will start implementing a base page object, which will be used by all other pages as a template. The base object will also provide regions that are blocks of functionality available for all other pages; for example, the search feature is available on all pages of the application. We will create a search region object that will be available for all the pages inherited from the base page. We will implement a class for the home page, which represents the home page of the application; search results page, which shows the list of products matching with the search criteria; and a product page, which provides attributes and actions related to a product. We will create a structure as shown in the following diagram:

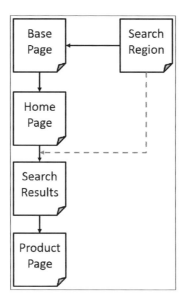

Organizing tests

Before we start implementing page objects for the sample application we are testing, let's implement a `BaseTestCase` class, which will provide us with the `setUp()` and `tearDown()` methods so that we don't need to write these for each test class we create. We can also put reusable code in this class. Create `basetestcase.py` and implement the `BaseTestCase` class as shown in the following code:

```
import unittest
from selenium import webdriver

class BaseTestCase(unittest.TestCase):
    def setUp(self):
```

```
        # create a new Firefox session
        self.driver = webdriver.Firefox()
        self.driver.implicitly_wait(30)
        self.driver.maximize_window()

        # navigate to the application home page
        self.driver.get('http://demo.magentocommerce.com/')

    def tearDown(self):
        # close the browser window
        self.driver.quit()
```

The BasePage object

The `BasePage` object will act as a parent object for all the page objects that we will create in our test suite. The base page provides common code that the page object can use. Let's create `base.py` and implement `BasePage` as shown in the following code:

```python
from abc import abstractmethod
class BasePage(object):
    """ All page objects inherit from this """

    def __init__(self, driver):
        self._validate_page(driver)
        self.driver = driver

    @abstractmethod
    def _validate_page(self, driver):
        return

    """ Regions define functionality available through
      all page objects """
    @property
    def search(self):
        from search import SearchRegion
        return SearchRegion(self.driver)

class InvalidPageException(Exception):
    """ Throw this exception when you don't find
      the correct page """
    pass
```

We added an abstract method called `_validate_page()`, which will be implemented by the page objects inheriting from `BasePage` to validate that the page they represent is loaded in the browser before the test can use attributes or actions.

We also created a property called `search` that returns the `SearchRegion` object. This is similar to a page object. However, `SearchRegion` represents the search box displayed on all the pages of the application. So, adding to each page object we are sharing this from the `BasePage` class.

We also implemented `InvalidPageException`, which is used in the `_validate_page()` method. If it fails to validate the page, `InvalidPageExecption` will be raised.

Implementing page objects

Now, let's start implementing page objects for each page that we're going to deal with in our test.

1. First we will define `HomePage`. Create `homepage.py` and implement the `HomePage` class as shown in the following code:

    ```
    from base import BasePage
    from base import InvalidPageException


    class HomePage(BasePage):

        _home_page_slideshow_locator =
          'div.slideshow-container'

        def __init__(self, driver):
            super(HomePage, self).__init__(driver)

        def _validate_page(self, driver):
            try:
                driver.find_element_by_class_name
                  (self._home_page_slideshow_locator)
            except:
                raise InvalidPageException
                  ("Home Page not loaded")
    ```

    One of the practices that we will follow is to separate the locator strings from the place where they are being used. We will create a private variable to store locators using the _ prefix. For example, the `_home_page_slideshow_locator` variable stores the locator for the slideshow component displayed on the home page of the application. We will use this to validate whether the browser is indeed showing the home page, as follows:

    ```
    _home_page_slideshow_locator = 'div.slideshow-container'
    ```

We also implemented the _validate_page() method in the HomePage class. This method validates whether the home page is loaded in the browser using the element used to display a slideshow on the home page.

2. Next, we will implement the SearchRegion class, which handle the search feature of the application. It provides the searchFor() method, which returns the SearchResult class representing the search results page. Create a new search.py file and implement both the classes as shown in the following code:

```python
from base import BasePage
from base import InvalidPageException
from product import ProductPage

class SearchRegion(BasePage):
    _search_box_locator = 'q'

    def __init__(self, driver):
        super(SearchRegion, self).__init__(driver)

    def searchFor(self, term):
        self.search_field =
            self.driver.find_element_by_name
            (self._search_box_locator)
        self.search_field.clear()
        self.search_field.send_keys(term)
        self.search_field.submit()
        return SearchResults(self.driver)

class SearchResults(BasePage):
    _product_list_locator  = 'ul.products-grid > li'
    _product_name_locator  = 'h2.product-name a'
    _product_image_link    = 'a.product-image'
    _page_title_locator    = 'div.page-title'


    _products_count = 0
    _products = {}

    def __init__(self, driver):
        super(SearchResults, self).__init__(driver)
        results = self.driver.find_elements_by_css_selector
            (self._product_list_locator)
        for product in results:
            name = product.find_element_by_css_selector
```

```
                    (self._product_name_locator).text
                self._products[name] =
                    product.find_element_by_css_selector
                    (self._product_image_link)

        def _validate_page(self, driver):
            if 'Search results for' not in driver.title:
                raise InvalidPageException
                    ('Search results not loaded')

        @property
        def product_count(self):
            return len(self._products)

        def get_products(self):
            return self._products

        def open_product_page(self, product_name):
            self._products[product_name].click()
            return ProductPage(self.driver)
```

3. Finally, we will implement the `ProductPage` class, which has some attributes related to a product. We can access a product from the `SearchResults` class, which has a method to open the product details page for a given product. Create a `product.py` file and implement the `ProductPage` class as shown in the following code:

```
from base import BasePage
from base import InvalidPageException

class ProductPage(BasePage):
    _product_view_locator          = 'div.product-view'
    _product_name_locator          = 'div.product-name
                                      span'
    _product_description_locator    = 'div.tab-content
                                      div.std'
    _product_stock_status_locator   = 'p.availability
                                      span.value'
    _product_price_locator          = 'span.price'

    def __init__(self, driver):
        super(ProductPage, self).__init__(driver)

    @property
    def name(self):
```

```
        return self.driver.\
            find_element_by_css_selector
              (self._product_name_locator)\
            .text.strip()

    @property
    def description(self):
        return self.driver.\
            find_element_by_css_selector
              (self._product_description_locator)\
            .text.strip()

    @property
    def stock_status(self):
        return self.driver.\
            find_element_by_css_selector
              (self._product_stock_status_locator)\
            .text.strip()

    @property
    def price(self):
        return self.driver.\
            find_element_by_css_selector
              (self._product_price_locator)\
            .text.strip()

    def _validate_page(self, driver):
        try:
            driver.find_element_by_css_selector
              (self._product_view_locator)
        except:
            raise InvalidPageException
              ('Product page not loaded')
```

You can further add actions on the product page to add a product to the shopping cart, or for comparison of products. Also, attributes that return the rating and other information related to the product are added back to the test.

Creating a test with page objects

Let's create a test that uses `BaseTestCase` and calls the page objects that we created to test the search feature of the application. This test creates an instance of the `HomePage` class and calls the `searchFor()` method, which returns an instance of `SearchResults`. Later, the test calls the `open_product_page()` method of the `SearchResults` class to open details for the specified product listed in the result. The test checks the attributes of a sample product. Create a `searchtest.py` file and implement the `SearchProductTest` test as shown in the following code:

```python
import unittest
from homepage import HomePage
from BaseTestCase import BaseTestCase

class SearchProductTest(BaseTestCase):
    def testSearchForProduct(self):
        homepage = HomePage(self.driver)
        search_results = homepage.search.searchFor('earphones')
        self.assertEqual(2, search_results.product_count)
        product = search_results.open_product_page
            ('MADISON EARBUDS')
        self.assertEqual('MADISON EARBUDS', product.name)
        self.assertEqual('$35.00', product.price)
        self.assertEqual('IN STOCK', product.stock_status)

if __name__ == '__main__':
    unittest.main(verbosity=2)
```

Notice that we did not write the `setUp()` and `tearDown()` methods in this test. We inherited this test class from `BaseTestCase`, which implements these methods. We can overload these methods if we want to do test-specific setup or clean-up.

In this example, we implemented page objects for search workflow navigation. You can also implement similar page objects or regions for shopping cart, account registration, login, and so on.

Summary

In this chapter, we recognized the need to write data-driven tests and organize the test code using the page object pattern for reusability, scalability, and maintainability. The data-driven pattern provides us the ability to separate test data from test case, so we can reuse the test code to test multiple test data. We also looked at how to use the `ddt` library along with `unittest` to implement data-driven testing and read data from various external sources. You learned the page object pattern and how it benefits in building a maintainable test suite by implementing page objects for the sample application and creating a test that uses the page objects.

In the next chapter you will learn some advanced techniques with Selenium WebDriver API, such as capturing screenshots and movies from test runs, performing mouse and keyboard actions, handling session cookies, and so on.

9

Advanced Techniques of Selenium WebDriver

So far in the book, we have seen how to set up Selenium WebDriver for testing web applications and some of the important features and APIs for locating and interacting with various elements in the browser.

In this chapter, we will explore some of the advanced APIs of Selenium WebDriver. These features come in handy when you're testing fairly complex applications.

In this chapter, you will learn more about:

- Creating tests that simulate keyboard or mouse events using the `Actions` class
- Simulating mouse operations such as drag-and-drop and double-click
- Running JavaScript code
- Capturing screenshots and movies of test runs
- Handling browser navigation and cookies

Methods for performing keyboard and mouse actions

The Selenium WebDriver's advanced user interactions API allows us to perform operations from simple keyboard and mouse events to complex mouse events such as drag-and-drop, pressing a hotkey combination, holding a key, and performing mouse operations. This is accomplished by using the `ActionChains` class in the Selenium WebDriver Python API.

Here is a list of the important methods supported by the `ActionChains` class for performing keyboard and mouse events:

Method	Description	Argument	Example
`click(on_element=None)`	This method performs the click operation.	`on_element`: This is the element to click. If None, clicks on the current mouse position.	`click(main_link)`
`click_and_hold(on_element=None)`	This method holds down the left mouse button on an element.	`on_element`: This is the element to click and hold down the mouse button. If None, clicks on current mouse position.	`click_and_hold(gmail_link)`
`double_click(on_element=None)`	This method performs a double-click on an element.	`on_element`: This is the element to double-click. If None, clicks on current mouse position.	`double_click(info_box)`
`drag_and_drop(source, target)`	This method performs the drag-and-drop operation.	`source`: This is the element to mouse down. `target`: The element to mouse up.	`drag_and_drop(img, canvas)`

Method	Description	Argument	Example

`key_down(value, element=None)`	This method sends a key press only, without releasing it. This should only be used with modifier keys (such as the *Ctrl*, *Alt*, and *Shift* keys).	key: This is the modifier key to send. Values are defined in the `Keys` class.
		
		`target:` The element to send keys. If `None`, sends a key to current focused element.
			`key_down(Keys. SHIFT)\`
			`send_keys('n')\`
			`key_up(Keys.SHIFT)`

`key_up(value, element=None)`	This method releases a modifier key.	key: This is the modifier key to send. Values are defined in the `Keys` class. `target:` This is the element to send keys. If `None`, sends a key to current focused element.	
`move_to_element(to_ element)`	This method moves the mouse to the middle of an element.	`to_ element:` This is the element to move to.	`move_to_ element(gmail_ link)`
`perform()`	This method performs all stored actions.		`perform()`

Method	Description	Argument	Example
`release(on_ element=None)`	This method releases a held mouse button.	`on_ element:` This is the element to mouse up	`release(banner_ img)`
`send_keys(keys_to_ send)`	This method sends keys to an element that has current focus.	`keys_to_ send:` This is the keys to send	`send_keys("hello")`
`send_keys_to_ element(element, keys_to_send)`	This method sends keys to an element.	`element:` This is the element to send keys. `keys_to_ send:` The keys to send.	`send_keys_to_ element(firstName, "John")`

For a detailed list visit `http://selenium.googlecode.com/git/docs/api/py/ webdriver/selenium.webdriver.common.action_chains.html`.

> The `Interactions` API is not supported on Safari. Also, there are limitations for certain events on various browsers. For more details, refer to `https://code.google.com/p/selenium/ wiki/AdvancedUserInteractions`.

Keyboard actions

Let's create a test that demonstrates how to use the keyboard actions such as pressing a hot key combination. In the sample app when we press the *Shift + N* key combination, a label will change its color, as shown in the following code:

```
from selenium import webdriver
from selenium.webdriver.common.by import By
from selenium.webdriver.support.ui import WebDriverWait
from selenium.webdriver.support import expected_conditions
from selenium.webdriver.common.action_chains import ActionChains
from selenium.webdriver.common.keys import Keys
import unittest


class HotkeyTest(unittest.TestCase):
```

```
URL = "https://rawgit.com/jeresig/jquery.hotkeys/
        master/test-static-05.html"

def setUp(self):
    self.driver = webdriver.Chrome()
    self.driver.get(self.URL)
    self.driver.implicitly_wait(30)
    self.driver.maximize_window()

def test_hotkey(self):
    driver = self.driver

    shift_n_label = WebDriverWait(self.driver, 10).\
        until(expected_conditions.visibility_of_element_
        located((By.ID, "_shift_n")))

    ActionChains(driver).\
        key_down(Keys.SHIFT).\
        send_keys('n').\
        key_up(Keys.SHIFT).perform()
    self.assertEqual("rgba(12, 162, 255, 1)",
                        shift_n_label.value_of_css_
                        property("background-color"))

def tearDown(self):
    self.driver.close()

if __name__ == "__main__":
    unittest.main(verbosity=2)
```

We can perform a hotkey press operation using the `ActionChains` class. In this example, we used a combination of `key_down()`, `send_key()`, and `key_up()` methods to perform *Shift* + *N* key press as if a real user has pressed these keys:

```
ActionChains(driver).\
    key_down(Keys.SHIFT).\
    send_keys('n').\
    key_up(Keys.SHIFT).perform()
```

The `ActionChains` class requires the `driver` instance to be passed. We can then arrange the sequence of events by calling the available methods and executing the action calling the `perform()` method.

The mouse movement

Here is another example that calls the mouse move event by calling the
move_to_element() method of the ActionChains class. This is equivalent to
the onMouseOver event. The move_to_element() method will move the mouse
cursor from its current location to the supplied element.

```python
from selenium import webdriver
from selenium.webdriver.common.by import By
from selenium.webdriver.support.ui import WebDriverWait
from selenium.webdriver.support import expected_conditions
from selenium.webdriver.common.action_chains import ActionChains
import unittest


class ToolTipTest (unittest.TestCase):
    def setUp(self):
        self.driver = webdriver.Firefox()
        self.driver.get("http://jqueryui.com/tooltip/")
        self.driver.implicitly_wait(30)
        self.driver.maximize_window()

    def test_tool_tip(self):
        driver = self.driver

        frame_elm = driver.find_element_by_class_name("demo-frame")
        driver.switch_to.frame(frame_elm)

        age_field = driver.find_element_by_id("age")
        ActionChains(self.driver).move_to_element(age_field).perform()

        tool_tip_elm = WebDriverWait(self.driver, 10)\
            .until(expected_conditions.visibility_of_element_
            located((By.CLASS_NAME, "ui-tooltip-content")))

        # verify tooltip message
        self.assertEqual("We ask for your age only for statistical
        purposes.", tool_tip_elm.text)

    def tearDown(self):
        self.driver.close()

if __name__ == "__main__":
    unittest.main(verbosity=2)
```

The double_click method

We can double-click on an element by calling the `double_click()` method of the `ActionChains` class in the following way:

```python
from selenium import webdriver

from selenium.webdriver.common.action_chains import ActionChains
import unittest

class DoubleClickTest (unittest.TestCase):
    URL = "http://api.jquery.com/dblclick/"

    def setUp(self):
        self.driver = webdriver.Chrome()
        self.driver.get(self.URL)
        self.driver.maximize_window()

    def test_double_click(self):
        driver = self.driver
        frame = driver.find_element_by_tag_name("iframe")
        driver.switch_to.frame(frame)
        box = driver.find_element_by_tag_name("div")

        # verify color is Blue
        self.assertEqual("rgba(0, 0, 255, 1)",
                        box.value_of_css_property("background-
color"))

        ActionChains(driver).move_to_element(
            driver.find_element_by_tag_name("span"))\
            .perform()

        ActionChains(driver).double_click(box).perform()

        # verify Color is Yellow
        self.assertEqual("rgba(255, 255, 0, 1)",
                        box.value_of_css_property("background-
color"))

    def tearDown(self):
        self.driver.close()

if __name__ == "__main__":
    unittest.main(verbosity=2)
```

The drag_and_drop method

In Selenium WebDriver, we can perform the drag-and-drop operation by calling the drag_and_drop() method of the ActionChains class. This method requires the source element that will be dragged, and the target element where the source element will be dropped. Here is an example of the drag_and_drop method:

```python
from selenium import webdriver
from selenium.webdriver.common.action_chains import ActionChains
import unittest


class DragAndDropTest (unittest.TestCase):

    URL = "http://jqueryui.com/resources/
          demos/droppable/default.html"

    def setUp(self):
        self.driver = webdriver.Firefox()
        self.driver.get(self.URL)
        self.driver.maximize_window(30)
        self.driver.maximize_window()

    def test_drag_and_drop(self):
        driver = self.driver

        source = driver.find_element_by_id("draggable")
        target = driver.find_element_by_id("droppable")

        ActionChains(self.driver).drag_and_drop(source, target).
        perform()
        self.assertEqual("Dropped!", target.text)

    def tearDown(self):
        self.driver.close()

if __name__ == "__main__":
    unittest.main(verbosity=2)
```

Executing JavaScript

We can execute JavaScript code through Selenium WebDriver using the methods available from the WebDriver class. This is useful when we cannot perform certain operations using the Selenium WebDriver API or we want to test the JavaScript code.

The WebDriver class provides the following methods to execute JavaScript code:

Method	Description	Argument	Example
execute_async_ script(script, *args)	This method asynchronously executes JavaScript in the current window/frame.	script: This is the JavaScript code args: This is any arguments for the JavaScript code	driver. execute_async_ script("return document.title")
execute_ script(script, *args)	This method synchronously executes JavaScript in the current window/frame.	script: This is the JavaScript code args: This is any arguments for the JavaScript code	driver.execute_ script("return document.title")

Let's create a test with a utility method, which highlights the elements before performing actions on these elements by using the JavaScript methods:

```python
from selenium import webdriver
import unittest


class ExecuteJavaScriptTest (unittest.TestCase):
    def setUp(self):
        # create a new Firefox session
        self.driver = webdriver.Firefox()
        self.driver.implicitly_wait(30)
        self.driver.maximize_window()

        # navigate to the application home page
        self.driver.get("http://demo.magentocommerce.com/")

    def test_search_by_category(self):

        # get the search textbox
        search_field = self.driver.find_element_by_name("q")
        self.highlightElement(search_field)
        search_field.clear()

        # enter search keyword and submit
        self.highlightElement(search_field)
```

```
        search_field.send_keys("phones")
        search_field.submit()

        # get all the anchor elements which have product names
        # displayed currently on result page using
        # find_elements_by_xpath method
        products = self.driver.find_elements_by_xpath("//h2[@
        class='product-name']/a")

        # check count of products shown in results
        self.assertEqual(2, len(products))

    def tearDown(self):
        # close the browser window
        self.driver.quit()

    def highlightElement(self, element):
        self.driver.execute_script("arguments[0].setAttribute('style',
        arguments[1]);",
        element, "color: green;
        border: 2px solid green;")
        self.driver.execute_script("arguments[0].setAttribute('style',
        arguments[1]);",
        element , "")

if __name__ == "__main__":
    unittest.main(verbosity=2)
```

We can execute the JavaScript code by calling the `execute_script` method of the `WebDriver` class, as shown in the following example. We can also pass arguments to the JavaScript code through this method. In this example, we are modifying the border style for a moment and reverting that change back. This will highlight the given element with green border during the execution. It is useful to know which step is being executed on screen:

```
    def highlightElement(self, element):
        self.driver.execute_script("arguments[0].setAttribute('style',
        arguments[1]);",
        element, "color: green; border: 2px solid green;")
        self.driver.execute_script("arguments[0].setAttribute('style',
        arguments[1]);",
        element , "")
```

Capturing screenshots of failures

Capturing screenshots during the test run comes very handy when you want to communicate failures to the developers. It also helps in debugging tests or creating evidence of the test run. Selenium WebDriver comes with built-in methods to capture screenshots during the test run. The `WebDriver` class provides the following methods to capture and save a screenshot:

Method	Description	Argument	Example

`Save_`
`screenshot(filename)`
	This method gets the screenshot of the current window and saves the image to the specified file.	`filename:` This is the path/name of the file to which the screenshot will be saved	`Driver.save_`
			`screenshot`
			`("homepage.png")`

`get_screenshot_as_`
`base64()`
	This method gets the screenshot of the current window as a base64 encoded string, which is useful in embedding images in HTML.		`driver.get_`
			`screenshot_as_`
			`base64()`

`get_screenshot_as_`
`file(filename)`
	This method gets the screenshot of the current window. It returns `False` if there is any IOError, else returns `True`. It uses full paths in your filename.	`filename:` This is the path/name of the file to which the screenshot will be saved	`driver.get_`
			`screenshot_as_`
			`file('/results/`
			`screenshots/`
			`HomePage.png')`

`get_screenshot_as_`
`png()`
	This method gets the screenshot of the current window as binary data.		`driver.get_`
			`screenshot_as_`
			`png()`

Let's create a test that captures a screenshot when it leads to failure. In this example, we'll locate an element that should be present on the application's home page. However, if the test doesn't find this element, it will throw NoSuchElementException and take a screenshot of the page displayed in the browser window, which we can use for debugging or sending to a developer as evidence.

```python
from selenium import webdriver
import datetime, time, unittest
from selenium.common.exceptions import NoSuchElementException


class ScreenShotTest(unittest.TestCase):
    def setUp(self):
        self.driver = webdriver.Firefox()
        self.driver.get("http://demo.magentocommerce.com/")

    def test_screen_shot(self):
        driver = self.driver
        try:
            promo_banner_elem = driver.find_element_by_id("promo_
            banner")
            self.assertEqual("Promotions", promo_banner_elem.text)
        except NoSuchElementException:
            st = datetime.datetime\
                .fromtimestamp(time.time()).strftime('%Y%m%d_%H%M%S')
            file_name = "main_page_missing_banner" + st + ".png"
            driver.save_screenshot(file_name)
            raise

    def tearDown(self):
        self.driver.close()

if __name__ == "__main__":
    unittest.main(verbosity=2)
```

In this example, when the test doesn't find the promotion banner element, it takes a screenshot using the save_screenshot() method. We need to pass the path and name of the file to which the resulting image will be saved, as shown:

```python
try:
    promo_banner_elem = driver.find_element_by_id("promo_banner")
    self.assertEqual("Promotions", promo_banner_elem.text)
except NoSuchElementException:
    st = datetime.datetime.fromtimestamp(time.time()).
strftime('%Y%m%d_%H%M%S')
    file_name = "main_page_missing_banner" + st + ".png"
    driver.save_screenshot(file_name)
    raise
```

While capturing and saving the screenshot, it is recommended to use unique names for the image files such as including a timestamp and also using the **Portable Network Graphics** (**PNG**) format for highest compression of the file, which also results in minimal file size.

Recording a video of the test run

Similar to capturing screenshots, recording a video of the test run helps in recording complete test sessions in a visual way. We can watch the recorded video to understand what happens during the test run. This can be used as evidence for other project stakeholders as well, or can also be used as demos.

Selenium WebDriver does not have built-in features to record video. Recording a video of the test run can be achieved by using a Python library called `Castro` separately. It was created by Jason Huggin, the creator of Selenium.

Castro is based on a cross-platform screen recording tool named **Pyvnc2swf** (refer to `http://www.unixuser.org/~euske/vnc2swf/pyvnc2swf.html`). It captures the screen where the tests are running using the VNC protocol and generates a **Shockwave Flash** (**SWF**) movie file.

Castro also allows recording sessions from a remote machine using the VNC protocol. It needs a VNC program installed on the machine to record the videos. Before installing Castro we need PyGame library to be installed. The PyGame package cannot be installed with pip command and we need to get PyGame installer from `http://www.pygame.org/download.shtml`.

We can install Castro using `pip` with the following command line:

```
pip install Castro
```

We also need to install or enable VNC on the desktop, where the tests will be executed. On Windows, we need to install a VNC program. **TightVNC** (`http://www.tightvnc.com/`) will be a good choice. Install the TightVNC server and viewer on Windows.

On Ubuntu, go to **Settings | Preference | Remote Desktop** and check the **Allow other users to view your desktop** checkbox. For Mac, we can install the Vine VNC server from `http://www.testplant.com/products/vine/` or enable **Remote Desktop** from **System Preferences**.

Let's capture a video recording of the search test case that we created in the earlier chapters, as shown in the following code:

```
import unittest
from selenium import webdriver
from castro import Castro
```

```python
class SearchProductTest(unittest.TestCase):
    def setUp(self):
        # create an instance of Castro and provide name for the output
        # file
        self.screenCapture = Castro(filename="testSearchByCategory.
        swf")
        # start the recording of movie
        self.screenCapture.start()

        # create a new Firefox session
        self.driver = webdriver.Firefox()
        self.driver.implicitly_wait(30)
        self.driver.maximize_window()

        # navigate to the application home page
        self.driver.get("http://demo.magentocommerce.com/")

    def test_search_by_category(self):

        # get the search textbox
        search_field = self.driver.find_element_by_name("q")
        search_field.clear()

        # enter search keyword and submit
        search_field.send_keys("phones")
        search_field.submit()

        # get all the anchor elements which have product names
        # displayed
        # currently on result page using find_elements_by_xpath method
        products = self.driver.find_elements_by_xpath("//h2[@
        class='product-name']/a")

        # check count of products shown in results
        self.assertEqual(2, len(products))

    def tearDown(self):
        # close the browser window
        self.driver.quit()
        # Stop the recording
        self.screenCapture.stop()

if __name__ == '__main__':
    unittest.main(verbosity=2)
```

To create a new video recording session, we need to create an Castro object and initialize the instance with the path and name of the capture file as an argument to the constructor. Screen capture is started with the `start()` method, which will record the entire screen until the `stop` method is called. Testing with the `setUp()` method is the best way to initialize the Castro instance and start the recording as shown in the following example:

```python
def setUp(self):
    #Create an instance of Castro and provide name for the output
    # file
    self.screenCapture = Castro(filename="testSearchByCategory.swf")
    # Start the recording of movie
    self.screenCapture.start()

    # create a new Firefox session
    self.driver = webdriver.Firefox()
    self.driver.implicitly_wait(30)
    self.driver.maximize_window()

    # navigate to the application home page
    self.driver.get("http://demo.magentocommerce.com/")
```

To stop the recording, call the `stop()` method. Again, the `teadDown()` method is a good place to call this method so that we can capture the entire test case, as shown in the following code:

```python
def tearDown(self):
    # close the browser window
    self.driver.quit()
    # Stop the recording
    self.screenCapture.stop()
```

If there are multiple tests in a class, we can initialize and stop the recording in the class level using the `setUp()` and `teardown()` methods instead of creating a new file for each test.

Handling pop-up windows

Testing pop-up windows involves identifying a pop-up window by its name attribute or window handle, switching the driver context to the desired pop-up window and then executing steps on the pop-up window, and finally switching back to the parent window.

When we create an instance of the browser from our tests, it is a parent window and any subsequent windows that are created from the parent window are called child windows or pop-up windows. We can work with any child window as long as it belongs to the current WebDriver context.

Here is an example of a pop-up window:

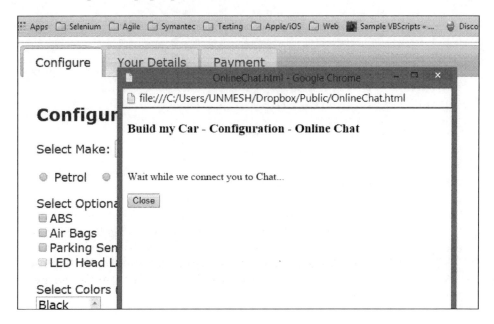

Create a new test class `PopupWindowTest` with the test method `test_popup_window()` as shown in the following code:

```python
from selenium import webdriver
import unittest


class PopupWindowTest(unittest.TestCase):

    URL = "https://rawgit.com/upgundecha/learnsewithpython/master/
        pages/Config.html"

    def setUp(self)     :
        self.driver = webdriver.Firefox()
        self.driver.get(self.URL)
        self.driver.maximize_window()

    def test_window_popup(self):
```

```
        driver = self.driver

        # save the WindowHandle of Parent Browser Window
        parent_window_id = driver.current_window_handle

        # clicking Help Button will open Help Page in a new Popup
        # Browser Window
        help_button = driver.find_element_by_id("helpbutton")
        help_button.click()
        driver.switch_to.window("HelpWindow")
        driver.close()
        driver.switch_to.window(parent_window_id)

    def tearDown(self):
        self.driver.close()

if __name__ == "__main__":
    unittest.main(verbosity=2)
```

Before the context is moved to the child window, we can save the handle of the parent window using the `current_window_handle` property. We will use this value later to switch back to the parent window from the child window. We can switch to the child window by using its name or window handle by calling the `switch_to.window()` method of the `WebDriver` class. In this example, we are using the name of the window, as shown:

```
driver.switch_to_window("HelpWindow")
```

After performing actions and checking on the help window, we can close it by calling the `close()` method and switch back to the parent window, as shown:

```
driver.close()

# switch back to Home page window using the handle
driver.switch_to_window(default_window)
```

Managing cookies

Cookies are important for any web applications to store information on the user's computer for a better user experience. Cookies are used to store user preferences, login information, and various other details of the client. The Selenium WebDriver API provides various methods to manage these cookies during testing. We can read cookie values, add cookies, and delete cookies during the test. This can be used to test how the application reacts when cookies are manipulated. The `WebDriver` class provides the following methods to manage cookies:

Method	Description	Argument	Example
`add_cookie(cookie_dict)`	This method adds a cookie to the current session	`cookie_dict:` This is a dictionary containing a cookie name and value pair	`driver.add_cookie({"foo","bar"})`
`delete_all_cookies()`	This method deletes all the cookies from the current session		`driver.delete_all_cookies()`
`delete_cookie(name)`	This method deletes a single cookie with the specified name	`name:` This is the name of the cookie to be deleted	`driver.delete_cookie("foo")`
`get_cookie(name)`	This method gets a single cookie by the name and returns the dictionary for the cookie if found, none, if not	`name:` This is the name of the cookie to search	`driver.get_cookie("foo")`
`get_cookies()`	This method gets a set of dictionaries corresponding to cookies from the current session		`driver.get_cookies()`

Here is an example that validates a cookie created to store the language selected by the user on the demo application's home page:

```python
import unittest
from selenium import webdriver
from selenium.webdriver.support.ui import Select


class CookiesTest(unittest.TestCase):
    def setUp(self):
        # create a new Firefox session
        self.driver = webdriver.Firefox()
        self.driver.implicitly_wait(30)
        self.driver.maximize_window()

        # navigate to the application home page
        self.driver.get("http://demo.magentocommerce.com/")

    def test_store_cookie(self):
        driver = self.driver
        # get the Your language dropdown as instance of Select class
        select_language = \
            Select(self.driver.find_element_by_id("select-language"))

        # check default selected option is English
        self.assertEqual("ENGLISH", select_language.first_selected_
        option.text)
        # store cookies should be none
        store_cookie = driver.get_cookie("store")
        self.assertEqual(None, store_cookie)

         # select an option using select_by_visible text
        select_language.select_by_visible_text("French")

        # store cookie should be populated with selected country
        store_cookie = driver.get_cookie("store")['value']
        self.assertEqual("french", store_cookie)

    def tearDown(self):
        # close the browser window
        self.driver.quit()

if __name__ == '__main__':
    unittest.main(verbosity=2)
```

We can retrieve the value of the cookie using the `get_cookie()` method of the `WebDriver` class. We need to pass the name of the cookie. This method returns a dictionary.

Summary

In this chapter, you learned about advanced features of Selenium WebDriver API for handling the keyboard and mouse events, capturing screenshots, recording videos, and handling cookies.

We used the `ActionChains` class to perform various keyboard and mouse operations. These features are very useful when dealing with applications that heavily use keyboard and mouse actions.

You saw how to run JavaScript code from your tests. This is a very powerful feature while dealing with applications that use Ajax and we can use the underlying JavaScript API from our scripts.

You captured screenshots for errors during test runs and also recorded a test session. This helps in debugging the tests as well as creating evidences for test runs.

Finally, you learned about the browser navigation methods and cookies.

In the next chapter, you will learn how to integrate our tests with other tools such as Continuous Integration tools to run the tests as part of the build process.

10
Integration with Other Tools and Frameworks

Selenium WebDriver Python API is very powerful and flexible. So far we have learned how Selenium WebDriver integrates with the `unittest` library and creates a simple testing framework. However, this does not limit us to just using the `unittest` library. We can integrate Selenium WebDriver with lots of other tools and frameworks. There are a number of ready-to-use frameworks available along with Selenium WebDriver.

We can use Selenium WebDriver for applying **Behavior-Driven Development (BDD)** in your projects with various frameworks that support BDD.

We can also integrate Selenium Python API with **Continuous Integration (CI)** and build tools that allow us to run the test immediately after the application is built. This provides an early feedback to developers about quality and stability of the application.

In this chapter, you will learn some of the major integration examples including:

- Downloading and installing Behave for BDD
- Writing features with Behave
- Automating features with Behave and Selenium WebDriver
- Downloading and installing Jenkins
- Setting up Jenkins to run Selenium tests
- Configuring Jenkins to capture results from test runs

Behavior-Driven Development

BDD is an agile software development method introduced by Dan North in his famous paper *Introducing BDD* (http://dannorth.net/introducing-bdd/).

BDD is also known as **Acceptance Test Driven Development (ATDD)**, story testing, or specification by example. BDD encourages collaboration between developers, QAs, and nontechnical or business users in a software project to define specifications and decide acceptance criteria by writing test cases in a natural language that nonprogrammers can read.

 There are a number of tools available in Python to implement BDD; the two major tools are **Behave** (https://pythonhosted.org/behave/) and **Lettuce** (http://lettuce.it/), which is inspired by the very famous BDD tool called **Cucumber** (http://cukes.info/) available in Ruby.

You will learn how to use Behave to implement BDD for the sample application in the upcoming sections.

Installing Behave

Installing Behave is a simple process. We can download and install Behave with the following command line:

```
pip install behave
```

This will download and install Behave along with its dependencies. There are additional installation options available for Behave at https://pythonhosted.org/behave/install.html.

Writing the first feature in Behave

The process starts with discussing and listing the features and user stories for these features for the application that is being developed. Various stakeholders meet together and create a list of features, user stories, and acceptance criteria in a ubiquitous language, which is understood by all the parties, including developers, testers, business analysts, and customers. Behave supports creating feature files in the Gherkin language in the **Given, When, Then (GWT)** format. Refer to https://github.com/cucumber/cucumber/wiki/Gherkin for more information on the Gherkin language.

Let's begin with a feature for the search functionality in the sample application. The search feature should enable users to search for products from the home page. The feature file provides a simple description for the user story and acceptance criteria as a scenario outline in the GWT format. These are also known as scenario steps, explained as follows:

- **Given**: This sets a precondition to execute the scenario; navigate to the home page in this scenario

- **When**: This contains the actions for the scenario; search for a term in this example

- **Then**: This contains the outcome of the scenario; check whether the list of matching products is displayed in this example

We can have multiple `When` and `Then` steps in a scenario:

```
Feature: I want to search for products

  Scenario Outline: Search
    Given I am on home page
     when I search for "phone"
     then I should see list of matching products in search results
```

To use this feature with Behave, we need to store this in a plain text file with a `.feature` extension. Let's create a folder named `bdd/feature` and save this file as `search.feature` in the folder.

Implementing a step definition file for the feature

Once we write the feature files, we need to create step definitions for the steps written in scenario outline. Step definitions are Python code blocks that understand the steps written in plain text format and contain the code to either call the API or Selenium WebDriver commands to execute the steps. The step definition files should be stored in a `steps` subfolder where feature files are stored. Let's create a `search_steps.py` file with the following step definitions:

```
from behave import *


@given('I am on home page')
def step_i_am_on_home_page(context):
    context.driver.get("http://demo.magentocommerce.com/")


@when('I search for {text}')
```

```
def step_i_search_for(context, text):
    search_field = context.driver.find_element_by_name("q")
    search_field.clear()

    # enter search keyword and submit
    search_field.send_keys(text)
    search_field.submit()


@then('I should see list of matching products in search results')
def step_i_should_see_list(context):
    products = context.driver.\
        find_elements_by_xpath("//h2[@class='product-name']/a")
    # check count of products shown in results
    assert len(products) > 0
```

For each GWT, we need to create a matching step definition. For example, for the given I am on home page step, we created the following step definition. Steps are identified using decorators that match the predicate from the feature file: @given, @when, and @then. The decorator accepts a string containing the rest of the phrase used in the scenario step it belongs to, in this case, I am on home page.

```
@given('I am on home page')
def step_i_am_on_home_page(context):
    context.driver.get("http://demo.magentocommerce.com/")
```

We can also pass parameters that are embedded in steps to the step definition. For example, for @when we are passing the search phrase as when I search for "phone".

We can read the value using {text} as shown in the following code sample:

```
@when('I search for {text}')
def step_i_search_for(context, text):
    search_field = context.driver.find_element_by_name("q")
    search_field.clear()

    # enter search keyword and submit
    search_field.send_keys(text)
    search_field.submit()
```

You can see the context variable passed to the step definitions. The context variable is used by Behave to store information to share around. It runs at three levels, automatically managed by Behave. We can also use the context variable to store and share information between the steps.

Creating environment configurations

Before we can run the feature, we need to create an environment file that is used to set up common Behave settings and any code that will be shared between steps or step definition files. This is a great place to initialize the WebDriver to start Firefox, which will be used to run the steps using the Selenium WebDriver. Create an `environment.py` file by the side of the feature files and add the `before_all()` and `after_all()` methods, which will be executed before and after the features are executed, as shown in the following code:

```
from selenium import webdriver

def before_all(context):
    context.driver = webdriver.Chrome()

def after_all(context):
    context.driver.quit()
```

Running features

Now, it's time to run the features with Behave. This is really simple. Navigate to the bdd folder that we created in the earlier steps and execute the behave command:

```
behave
```

Behave will execute all the features that are written in the bdd folder. It will use the step definition and environment settings that we made to run the scenarios. At the end of execution, you will see a summary of the execution, as shown in the following screenshot:

Behave generates a summary at three levels, namely features, scenarios, and steps for pass and failure.

Using a scenario outline

Sometimes we might want to run scenario(s) with a number of variables giving a set of known states, actions to take, and expected outcomes, all using the same steps, something similar to data-driven tests. We can use a scenario outline for this.

Let's rewrite the `search.feature` file with a scenario outline and examples as given in the following steps. The scenario outline works like a template, for example, given in the `Example` section.

1. In this example, we create two examples to check the search functionality on the categories or for a specific product. The `Example` sections contain the search term and the expected results in a tabular format:

   ```
   Feature: I want to search for products

     Scenario Outline: Search
       Given I am on home page
         when I search for <term>
         then I should see results <search_count> in search results

     Examples: By category
         | term      | search_count |
         | Phones    | 2            |
         | Bags      | 7            |

     Examples: By product name
         | term           | search_count |
         | Madison earbuds | 3           |
   ```

2. Also, modify the `search_steps.py` file to match the text used in steps:

   ```python
   from behave import *


   @given('I am on home page')
   def step_i_am_on_home_page(context):
       context.driver.get("http://demo.magentocommerce.com/")


   @when('I search for {text}')
   def step_i_search_for(context, text):
       search_field = context.driver.find_element_by_name("q")
       search_field.clear()

       # enter search keyword and submit
   ```

```
        search_field.send_keys(text)
        search_field.submit()


    @then('I should see results {text} in search results')
    def step_i_should_see_results(context, text):
        products = context.driver.\
            find_elements_by_xpath("//h2[@class='product-name']/a")
        # check count of products shown in results
        assert len(products) >= int(text)
```

When we execute this feature, Behave will automatically repeat the scenario outline for the number of rows it finds in the `Example` section that are written in the `search.feature` file. It passes the data from the example data to the scenario steps and executes the definition. You can see the outcome after Behave is run on the modified feature. Behave prints all the combinations it ran on the feature as shown in following screenshot:

```
C:\Users\amitr\Desktop\setests_final\bdd>behave
Feature: I want to search for products # features\search.feature:1

  Scenario Outline: Search                       # features\search.feature:3
    Given I am on home page                      # steps\search_steps.py:4
    When I search for Phones                     # steps\search_steps.py:9
    Then I should see results 2 in search results # steps\search_steps.py:18

  Scenario Outline: Search                       # features\search.feature:3
    Given I am on home page                      # steps\search_steps.py:4
    When I search for Bags                       # steps\search_steps.py:9
    Then I should see results 7 in search results # steps\search_steps.py:18

  Scenario Outline: Search                       # features\search.feature:3
    Given I am on home page                      # steps\search_steps.py:4
    When I search for Madison earbuds            # steps\search_steps.py:9
    Then I should see results 3 in search results # steps\search_steps.py:18

1 feature passed, 0 failed, 0 skipped
3 scenarios passed, 0 failed, 0 skipped
9 steps passed, 0 failed, 0 skipped, 0 undefined
Took 0m14.539s

C:\Users\amitr\Desktop\setests_final\bdd>
```

 Behave also supports report generation in JUnit format using the `-junit` switch.

CI with Jenkins

Jenkins is a popular CI server written in Java. It is derived from the Hudson project. Both Jenkins and Hudson provide similar features.

Jenkins supports various version control tools such as CVS, SVN, Git, Mercurial, Perforce, and ClearCase, and can execute projects built with Apache Ant or Maven for Java. However, it can also build projects for other platforms using plugins, arbitrary shell scripts, and Windows' batch commands.

Apart from building the software, Jenkins can be deployed to set up an automated testing environment where Selenium WebDriver tests can be run unattended based on a defined schedule, or every time changes are submitted to the version control system.

In the upcoming sections, you will learn how to set up Jenkins to run tests using a free-style project template.

Preparing for Jenkins

Before we start using Jenkins to run our tests, we need to make few changes so that we can take advantage of Jenkins's capabilities. We will use Jenkins to run our tests on a pre-defined schedule and collect results from tests so that Jenkins can show them on a dashboard. We will reuse smoke tests that we created in *Chapter 2, Writing Tests Using unittest*.

We used the TestSuite runner of unittest to execute the bunch of tests together. We will now output the results of these tests in the JUnit report format. For this, we need a Python library called xmlrunner from https://pypi.python.org/pypi/xmlrunner/1.7.4.

Download and install xmlrunner with the following command line:

pip install xmlrunner

We will use smoketests.py, which uses the TestSuite runner to run the tests from homepagetests.py and searchtest.py. We will use the xmlrunner.XML TestRunner to run these tests and generate a test report in JUnit format. This report will be generated in XML format and kept in the test-reports subfolder. To use xmlrunner, please make the highlighted changes in smoketest.py, as shown in the following code example:

```
import unittest
from xmlrunner import xmlrunner
from searchtest import SearchProductTest
from homepagetests import HomePageTest
```

```
# get all tests from SearchProductTest and HomePageTest class
search_tests = unittest.TestLoader().loadTestsFromTestCase(SearchProd
uctTest)
home_page_tests = unittest.TestLoader().loadTestsFromTestCase(HomePag
eTest)

# create a test suite combining search_test and home_page_test
smoke_tests = unittest.TestSuite([home_page_tests, search_tests])

# run the suite
xmlrunner.XMLTestRunner(verbosity=2, output='test-reports').run(smoke_
tests)
```

Setting up Jenkins

Setting up Jenkins is fairly straightforward. You can download and install Jenkins using the installers available for various platforms. In following example, we will set up Jenkins and create a new build job to run the smoke tests on the sample application:

1. Download and install the Jenkins CI server from `http://jenkins-ci.org/`. For this recipe, the Jenkins Windows installer is used to set up Jenkins on a Windows 7 machine.

2. Navigate to **Jenkins Dashboard** (`http://localhost:8080` by default) in the browser window.

3. On **Jenkins Dashboard**, click on **New Item** or **create new jobs** link to create a new Jenkins job as shown in the following screenshot:

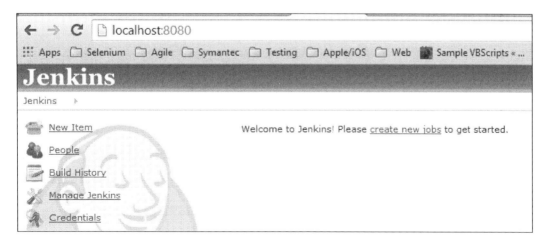

4. Enter `Demo_App_Smoke_Test` in the **Item name** textbox and select the **Build a free-style software project** radio button as shown in the following screenshot:

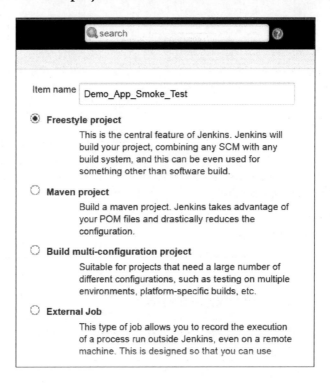

5. Click on the **OK** button. A new job will be created with the specified name.

> We can connect to various version control or **Source Control Management (SCM)** tools such as SVN, GIT, Perforce, and so on to store the source and test code. We can then get the latest version of the code to build and test the software in the Jenkins workspace as part of building the steps. However, to keep things simple, in this example, we will copy the test scripts from a folder to the Jenkins workspace using the **Execute Windows batch command** build step as described in following set of steps.

6. In the **Build** section, click on **Add build step** and select the **Execute Windows batch command** option from the dropdown.

7. Enter the following command in the **Command** textbox as shown in the following screenshot. Paths will be different in your case. This command will copy the Python files containing smoke tests to the Jenkins workspace and run `smoketest.py` as shown:

```
copy c:\setests\chapter10\smoketests\*.py
```

```
python smoketest.py
```

8. We configured `smoketest.py` to generate test results in JUnit format so that Jenkins can display the test results on its dashboard. To integrate these reports with Jenkins, click on **Add post-build action** and select the **Publish JUnit test result report** option from the dropdown as shown in the following screenshot:

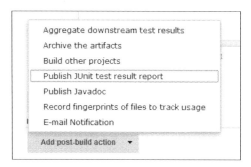

9. In the **Post-build Actions** section, add `test-reports/*.xml` in the **Test report XMLs** textbox as shown in the following screenshot. Every time Jenkins runs the tests, it will read test results from the `test-report` subfolder.

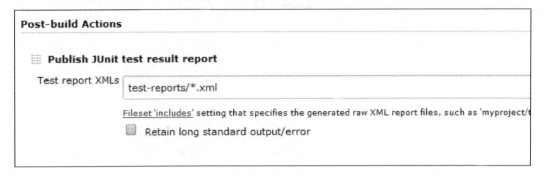

10. To schedule tests for automatic execution in the **Build Triggers** section, select **Build periodically** and enter the data as shown in the following screenshot in the **Schedule** textbox. This will trigger the build process every day at 10 p.m. and Jenkins will run the tests as part of the build process unattended so you can see the results next morning when you arrive at the office.

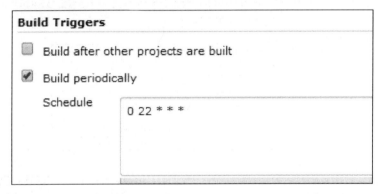

11. Click on the **Save** button to save the job configuration. Jenkins will display the project page for the newly created job.

12. We can check if everything is set to see if tests are executed. Click on the **Build Now** link to run the job manually as shown in the following screenshot:

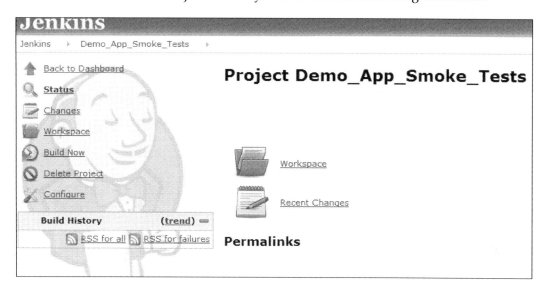

13. You can see the running status for the build in the **Build History** section as shown in the following screenshot:

14. Click on the running item in the **Build History** section, which will open the following page:

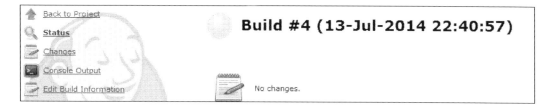

15. Apart from the status on Jenkins and the progress bar, we can also see what's happening behind the scenes by opening the **Console Output** link. This will open the **Console Output** page with the command-line output as shown in the following screenshot:

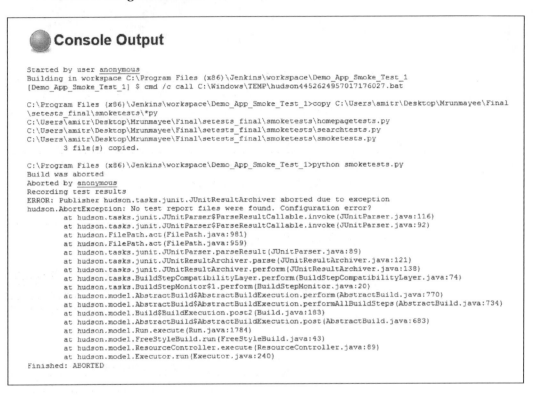

16. Once the build process is completed by Jenkins, we can see a build page similar to the one shown in the next screenshot.

17. Jenkins displays test results and various other metrics by reading the result files generated by the `unittest` frameworks. Jenkins also archives test results. To view the test results, click on the **Test Results** link on the build page.

18. We configured our tests to generate the test results in the JUnit format and when we click on **Test Results**, Jenkins will display the JUnit test results as shown in the following screenshot. It highlights the tests that are failed and a summary for the tests.

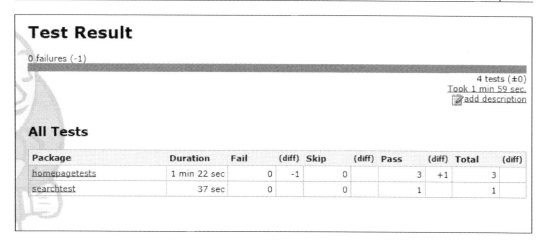

19. We can drill down by clicking on the package names and see the results for individual tests as shown in the following screenshot:

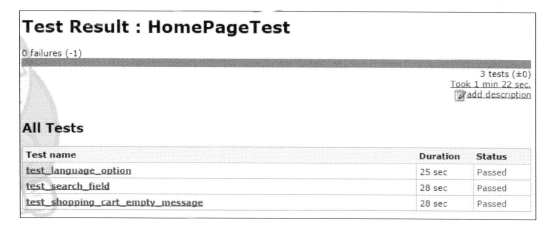

Jenkins also shows a status on the Dashboard for the job with the status of the last build in the following format:

Summary

In this chapter, you learned how to integrate Selenium with Behave for BDD and Jenkins for CI. You saw how to integrate Selenium WebDriver API with Behave to run automated acceptance tests by writing features and step definition files.

You set up Jenkins to run Selenium WebDriver tests so that you can run these tests while building the software or scheduling tests so they can be run nightly. Jenkins provides an easy-to-set-up model to run the build and test jobs for various application development platforms and environments.

This completes your learning journey using Selenium WebDriver with Python. You learned some basic lessons on using Selenium WebDriver to automate browser interaction to create automated tests for web applications. You can use this knowledge and build your own testing framework.

Index

L

Lettuce, BDD tool
  URL 178
links
  finding 61
  finding, partial text used 62
lists
  working with 79, 80
locators
  finding, developer tools used 47

M

Mac OS X
  with Safari 113, 114
Magento
  URL 18
maximize_window() method 70
Mobile web apps 122
mouse movement
  about 162
  double_click method 163
  drag_and_drop method 164
  performing 157
move_to_element(to_element) method 159

N

name attribute
  used, for finding elements 55
name property 69
native apps 122
nodes
  adding 111
  Chrome node, adding 113
  Firefox node, adding 112
  IE node, adding 111, 112
nose framework 31

O

options property 81
orientation property 69

P

page object pattern
  about 148, 149
  BasePage object 150, 151
  implementing 151-154
  test, creating with 155
  tests, organizing 149
pages
  inspecting, Google Chrome used 49, 50
  inspecting, Internet Explorer used 50, 51
  inspecting with Firefox, Firebug add-in
      used 47, 48
page_source property 69
partial text
  used, for finding links 62
perform() method 159
pip installer tool
  URL 8
pop-up windows
  handling 171-173
  working with 84
**Portable Network Graphics (PNG)
      format 169**
**presence_of_all_elements_located(locator)
      condition 95**
**presence_of_element_located(locator)
      condition 95**
properties and methods
  URL 69, 71, 80
PyCharm
  about 10, 12
  setting up 15-17
  URL 11
PyCharm Community Edition
  URL 15
PyDev
  URL 12
PyDev Eclipse plugin 12
PyScripter 13
pytest framework
  URL 31
Python
  installing 8

Thank you for buying
Learning Selenium Testing Tools with Python

About Packt Publishing

Packt, pronounced 'packed', published its first book, *Mastering phpMyAdmin for Effective MySQL Management*, in April 2004, and subsequently continued to specialize in publishing highly focused books on specific technologies and solutions.

Our books and publications share the experiences of your fellow IT professionals in adapting and customizing today's systems, applications, and frameworks. Our solution-based books give you the knowledge and power to customize the software and technologies you're using to get the job done. Packt books are more specific and less general than the IT books you have seen in the past. Our unique business model allows us to bring you more focused information, giving you more of what you need to know, and less of what you don't.

Packt is a modern yet unique publishing company that focuses on producing quality, cutting-edge books for communities of developers, administrators, and newbies alike. For more information, please visit our website at www.packtpub.com.

About Packt Open Source

In 2010, Packt launched two new brands, Packt Open Source and Packt Enterprise, in order to continue its focus on specialization. This book is part of the Packt Open Source brand, home to books published on software built around open source licenses, and offering information to anybody from advanced developers to budding web designers. The Open Source brand also runs Packt's Open Source Royalty Scheme, by which Packt gives a royalty to each open source project about whose software a book is sold.

Writing for Packt

We welcome all inquiries from people who are interested in authoring. Book proposals should be sent to author@packtpub.com. If your book idea is still at an early stage and you would like to discuss it first before writing a formal book proposal, then please contact us; one of our commissioning editors will get in touch with you.

We're not just looking for published authors; if you have strong technical skills but no writing experience, our experienced editors can help you develop a writing career, or simply get some additional reward for your expertise.

Selenium WebDriver Practical Guide

ISBN: 978-1-78216-885-0   Paperback: 264 pages

Interactively automate web applications using Selenium WebDriver

1. Covers basic to advanced concepts of WebDriver.

2. Learn how to design a more effective automation framework.

3. Explores all the APIs within WebDriver.

4. Acquire an in-depth understanding of each concept through practical code examples.

Selenium Testing Tools Cookbook

ISBN: 978-1-84951-574-0   Paperback: 326 pages

Over 90 recipes to build, maintain, and improve test automation with Selenium WebDriver

1. Learn to leverage the power of Selenium WebDriver with simple examples that illustrate real-world problems and their workarounds.

2. Each sample demonstrates key concepts allowing you to advance your knowledge of Selenium WebDriver in a practical and incremental way.

3. Explains testing of mobile web applications with Selenium Drivers for platforms such as iOS and Android.

Please check **www.PacktPub.com** for information on our titles

Selenium 2 Testing Tools Beginner's Guide

ISBN: 978-1-84951-830-7   Paperback: 232 pages

Learn to use Selenium testing tools from scratch

1. Automate web browsers with Selenium WebDriver to test web applications.

2. Set up Java Environment for using Selenium WebDriver.

3. Learn good design patterns for testing web applications.

Instant Selenium Testing Tools Starter

ISBN: 978-1-78216-514-9   Paperback: 52 pages

A short, fast, and focused guide to Selenium Testing tools that delivers immediate results

1. Learn something new in an Instant! A short, fast, and focused guide delivering immediate results.

2. Learn to create web tests using Selenium tools.

3. Learn to use page object pattern.

4. Run and analyse test results on an easy-to-use platform.

Please check **www.PacktPub.com** for information on our titles

24146921R00121

Made in the USA
Middletown, DE
16 September 2015